ENTER
laughing

THE EARLY YEARS

by Neil Crone

ĕß

echo
BOOKS

An imprint of
Wintertickle **PRESS**

Enter Laughing: The Early Years

ISBN 978-1-894813-62-4

Published by Echo Books, an imprint of Wintertickle Press
92 Caplan Avenue, Suite 155
Barrie, ON, Canada   L4N 0Z7

WinterticklePress.com
facebook.com/WintertticklePress

echo
ʙᴏᴏᴋs

An imprint of

Wintertickle **PRESS**

To my wonderful, wonky, beautiful family and families everywhere…
you are the glue that holds us all together on this little blue ball.

COVER PHOTO CREDIT

The cover photo was graciously taken by Rob Johnson. For more information or inquiries about Rob Johnson's photography, please contact him via email at bobstate@me.com.

ACKNOWLEDGEMENT FROM NEIL CRONE

With love and heartfelt appreciation for my editors, publishers and all the wonderful people who have made these little columns possible. And special thanks to anyone who ever opened a paper and looked for my face. I am in your debt.

NOTES ABOUT ORIGINAL COLUMNS

These columns were originally published in select Metroland newspapers. Both content and style have been edited from the original to better suit the book format.

Contents

It's funny how life works in mysterious ways. So often, you think some event, epiphany or milestone is the goal only to find out that it was merely a stepping stone towards a better, bigger plan. Isn't retrospection great?

The road to this collection of articles is as serendipitous as it gets. Throughout the years, I watched Neil Crone, Canadian actor, in a variety of television shows, movies and commercials without even so much as knowing his name. But, there was a knowing just the same. Every time I saw him, I would think "there's that guy again." He seemed strangely familiar and comfortable.

Little did I know that we would one day meet, due in part to my new-found addiction to running. In middle age and in need of a new hobby, I decided to take up distance running. Although running in middle age is a myriad of things—it is mostly funny. At least from where I was sitting—or stepping so to speak.

In my youth I had written a few humour books and always appreciated a good chuckle so I started to blog about my crazy experiences and called it *The Moose Pyjama Chronicles: Confessions of a Middle Aged Woman*. Needless to say I was excited when my following grew to a whopping 37 people, including my mom, dad, kids and extended family.

While visiting my parents, my father said, "I read your blog. It was funny. It reminds me a bit of Neil Crone, the guy who writes for our local paper."

My curiosity was piqued and my dad sent me an article that Neil had written about the foibles of technology. I laughed and then I laughed some more. Not only was it funny; it was the best kind of funny—it was true.

I ended up contacting Neil and we worked together on producing his children's book aptly titled *Who Farted? Stories in Verse for Big & Little Kids.* It was a great experience. When I told my father about the project he was excited. But, I could see the wheels turning in his head, "You should publish an anthology of his articles. People would love to read a collections of his columns."

My father, the unwitting conduit in this meandering maze, connected the many pieces together. I love the synchronicity of life that naturally and mysteriously unfolds—but somehow always works out.

Whenever I talk to people who read Neil Crone's newspaper columns, the comments always carry the same themes. Recurring adjectives include insightful, thoughtful, sensitive, down-to-earth and just plain funny. Many have their theories on why his writing is so popular. My theory is simple. I believe that the columns, once dissected, have one thing we all crave—authenticity. Personally, I enjoy and sense the genuineness in each and every article and know you will too.

- Heather Down, publisher, Wintertickle Press
and author of *Postcards from Space: The Chris Hadfield Story*

INTRODUCTION

Enter Laughing would never have come about were it not for the magic of *Harry Potter*. Fourteen years ago I was living in the little village of Sunderland, Ontario, working primarily as an actor and scribbling a little bit of children's poetry now and then, mostly as a way to creatively kill the downtime in between auditions and gigs. Although I certainly enjoyed writing and always had, I wouldn't and couldn't exactly call myself a writer. The *Harry Potter* phenomenon had just begun to get a good head of steam back then. I remember wonderful hours spent reading those books aloud to both of my boys, all of us completely lost in their magic. And the magic wasn't just in the story lines. J.K. Rowling was casting an incredibly potent spell on a whole generation of children—she was getting kids reading. I loved her and those books for that.

Which was why, when I read a letter to the editor in a local community paper, denouncing *Harry Potter* and all things Hogwarts, I had to write a rebuttal.

With tongue firmly planted in cheek, I wrote my own letter to the editor responding to this silliness and I guess it must have struck a chord with people. The editor emailed me back telling me how much mail they'd received about my response. Out of the blue—magically, you might say—he asked me how I might feel about writing a monthly humour column. Just as magically, I said that would be great—and *Enter Laughing* was born.

From those once a month, 500-word, limited-circulation submissions, this little column has grown into a weekly, syndicated and, I am very proud to say, award-winning column. More than that, it has become one of the most treasured things in my life. Not a week goes by that I don't hear something, sometimes negative, usually wonderfully positive about something I've written. I can't tell you how nice that is. How fantastic it feels to know that something you've thought about, some few words that seemed important to you, were resonating in a special way with other people.

I have been lucky enough to have been the recipient of a number of awards and accolades throughout my career. All of them have felt good. But the highest, best and most important award I have ever been accorded is the first time a reader told me she cut my columns out and placed them on her fridge. I think even *Harry Potter* would find that pretty magical.

"Laughter is the shortest distance between two people."

-Victor Borge (1909-2000)

I would like to know exactly when the first snowfall of the winter stopped being the bright harbinger of Christmas magic and started being the dark omen of an extra half-hour commuting time for me. I hate that. I hate when I let magic fall out of my life.

It can happen so easily and so quickly it's almost unconscious. One minute you're a kid delighting in snowball fights and building forts, the next you're scowling behind the wheel with a jumbo gherkin up your backside. But I guess magic is like that, isn't it? It's like quicksilver. If you try to hold it in your hands it almost immediately changes shape and vanishes. It's still there, but you have to look for it. We constantly have to look for it.

In that respect children have it all over us adults. Having a kid around is like having a water witch for magic. They can smell it a mile away and the closer they get to it the more twitchy they become. Children's magic is infectious too; it's also free for the asking.

Not looking forward to putting the Christmas lights up again? Do it with your kids. Decorating the tree becoming a bit of a chore? Do it with your kids. I can't tell you how many times my own boys have saved me from becoming a Grinch. And not just around the holiday season either.

Once, toward the end of a particularly dark and frustrating day, I walked into our upstairs bathroom. Something on the wall caught my eye. There, a good eight feet off the ground, smeared along the wallpaper was a huge glob of toothpaste. I went from zero to crabby in no time flat.

I bellowed for the boys to come here. They appeared almost instantly, the tone of my voice telling them something was obviously rotten in Denmark.

Wordlessly, I pointed to the fluoride blob on the wall. They looked from me, to the wall, then to each other. There was a short pause, then both broke out laughing hysterically. Magic. My dark spell was broken.

They, with their wondrous radar for the ridiculous had seen how impossibly hilarious it was that someone their size could accidentally fling that much toothpaste that high. In that magical moment I saw it too and laughed my head off. They had saved me once again. My magic compass was back on course.

Very fortunately for all of us, children are not the only practitioners of magic in our world. We all have the power to enchant. Witness how remarkably transforming your own smile is to a stranger, how warm and wonderful a friend's hand feels on your shoulder as he greets you.

Simple things yes, but so very powerful—and all within everyone's ability.

I have learned one of the best ways to keep the magic from slipping out of my own life is to try and put some into someone else's. A friend once told me by complimenting her on her new hairdo, I had made her entire day.

Now if that isn't magic folks, I don't know what is.

If This Is Canada, Where's the Snow?

I know there are many of you out there who are loving the lack of cold temperatures and snow we are experiencing this winter, but it's killing me.

My philosophy has always been, if we're going to have winter, replete with snow and cold, then bring it on baby. Otherwise, why live here? Why not move to somewhere like Vancouver where it's green all year round? And while I personally find the concept of perpetually living in one season boring, at least it's a firm choice. You see, to me, you're either in or you're out—none of this halfway business. So far this has been the Barry Manilow of winters.

Normally by this point, halfway through January, I'd have already thrown my back out three or four times tobogganing. I'd have built a warren of snow tunnels and hideouts in the backyard to make the Viet Cong green with envy. I'd have surely been in the doghouse at least twice for accidentally nailing one of the children in the eye during a snowball fight. And my ice rink? Well, we won't go there again.

Of course it's been taking its toll on the kids as well. Pity the poor little sucker who got stiffed with new skis or a new sled for Christmas. Somewhere, I am sure, there's a kid or two, at the end of their hyper-active ropes, tobogganing down the broadloomed stairs. Can you blame them? As a parent I even feel guilty telling the kids to go outside and play in this lousy weather because for once, "There really is nothing to do!" What are they gonna do, build a mudman? Have a noball fight?

Even the people who normally hate winter seem to be peeved. Most of them have sunk a lot of cash into expensive Florida getaways and exotic cruises to escape the frozen hell of this season. How many of them are shaking their sun-hatted heads as they drive to Pearson International in plus 15 degree weather, staring resentfully at expensive boarding passes and wondering why they didn't buy that big-screen TV instead? After all, where's the fun in going away if you can't lie on the beach picturing your neighbour back home digging out from under a six-foot dump of wet snow?

And of course, what about the saddest cases of all—the snowmobilers? I personally know a large number of nearly suicidal people who have some very expensive hardware gathering dust in their garages. Can't you just picture these poor folks, sitting at their kitchen tables late into the night, wearing their new helmets and leafing disconsolately through their owner's manuals? Breaks your heart, doesn't it?

Anyway, I think it's pretty clear that, like it or not, snow and cold are necessary elements for a peaceful, happy existence in this province. Whether you're looking to get into it or away from it, we have to have it first.

SPRING BIKE RIDES SPAWN LEGENDS

Forget about Robin Redbreast, as far as I'm concerned, spring doesn't really arrive until you see kids tooling around on their bikes. Remember that first bike ride of the season? How good it felt, after a winter of lumbering around in a down-filled straightjacket, to feel that warm air whipping past your face as you cruised effortlessly downhill, going so fast the wind sucked the gob out of your mouth. That's living, friend.

Of course riding a bike has always had its attendant dangers. Inevitably the kid on the bike will fall off the bike. I need to make an important clarification here, however. There are two ways of falling off a bike. There is the *accident* and there is the *wipeout*. And there is a world of difference between the two—ask any kid.

For starters you *have* an accident. An accident is something totally catastrophic that you appear to have no control over. It's generally something that hurts a lot and allows you to cry in front of your pals. It is usually followed by some ashen-faced second or third party mournfully murmuring a phrase like, "Mrs. Crone you better come quick, Neil had an accident."

On the other hand you *take* a wipeout. A wipeout is essentially the same thing as an accident only there happen to be girls around. It still hurts like hell but crying is not allowed and at the end of the wipeout, the bleeding and scraped participant stands up from the wreckage and, in a voice loud enough for the females present to hear, boldly proclaims, "Whoa! You guys see that wipeout I just took?"

A spectacular bike wipeout is the stuff of legends. In the brief seconds it takes to nut yourself on your handlebars or do a face plant into a rosebush, a hero can be born.

How well I recall the ill-fated ride of Normy Richards down the steep side of Bridlewood Hill. The steep side of Bridlewood Hill was a long, hardpacked dirt autobahn that screamed downhill at a 45 degree angle of death and culminated in a curved tarmac lip. If a kid hit that lip at full speed he could get serious air—and the respect of every kid watching.

Well, a nervous Normy Richards came hurtling down the hill that day. He was mounted on his brother's bike, which was two sizes too big for starters, and the enormous wheels on that thing took him to speeds none of us had even dreamed about. Halfway down, in an incredible display of either raw courage or sheer stupidity, his feet left the pedals and consequently he lost any hope of slowing down. Seconds later Normy hit the paved lip and sailed gloriously into the air and into history. For at the apex of his flight, just when we thought he could not possibly trump himself, his front wheel flew off. He was still a good five feet off the ground.

Normy Richards was a walking scab for well over a month. But the legend of his bike wipeout will live forever.

Too Much Protection

On a walk through the schoolyard recently I noticed large circles of orange spray paint on the snow which seemed to demarcate or cordon off certain areas from others. Upon inquiry, my children explained to me the areas enclosed by the orange lines indicated private sanctuaries where groups of kids had built snow forts. According to the boys, only the kids who were working on or who had built the forts were allowed inside each boundary, thereby effectively quashing any planned fort-wrecking raids by rival clans. The lines were strictly teacher-enforced too—sort of a snow fort demilitarized zone.

I shook my head. What gives? This is a schoolyard for Pete's sake, not the West Bank. Who was the genius who came up with this one? Must we take the edges off every aspect of our children's lives? First there was the mad rush to dismantle any schoolyard structure that any kid had ever gotten a scab near. Then came the litany of litigation-proofing all recess games involving any kind of running, bouncing, hurling or jostling to the point where a game of tag was now played at a fast walk—and now this.

Ask any kid and they will tell you the whole point of building any snow structure is to eventually have it wrecked, either by hordes of marauding enemies or by oneself, to prevent said fort from falling into the hands of said enemies. The game is not finished until the fort is in ruins and someone is in tears. That's just how you play. If you don't like the rules, don't build the fort.

How, for goodness' sake, is a young boy to let a young girl know he likes her anymore? He can't pull her hair or steal her backpack or wreck her fort. What's he supposed to do? Email her? When we take the risk out of our lives we take away the potential for wonderful things. Things like courage, loyalty, fortitude and yes, forgiveness.

Never underestimate how much moxie it takes for a kid to suck up getting hit in the puss with an iceball in front of his pals or to come to the aid of a fallen chum in a snowball fight against overwhelming numbers. And have we forgotten how much courage is involved in the simple act of choosing sides in a fight? Or the brains it takes to negotiate your way out of one before an adult shows up? These are huge moments in our children's lives and we do them a grave injustice by removing them. Let our kids paint their days in bold, broad brush strokes of primary colours, not in watered down, inoffensive beiges.

By all means, teach them until you're blue in the face about road safety, strangers, bullying, tobacco, and drugs. Show them the stink of bigotry and intolerance wherever you encounter it. And above all, warn them about watching any Keanu Reeves film. But then, let them be. They will work the rest out on their own, amongst their own. We did.

We're Suckers for the Con Artists in Life

I'm a big believer in karma, you know, you reap what you sow and what goes around comes around? I just sometimes wish it would come around a little quicker.

I've been doing the math lately and it seems I get taken for a pretty good mark a lot of the time. I'm not a very good grown-up, I'm afraid. I lack the cynic gene. You know that skeptical, suspicious safety mechanism that prevents most adults from saying things like "Sure, I'll pay you up front" or "Yeah, I guess a handshake will do" or the ubiquitous "Sounds good to me, where do I sign?" I am sure I have said all those things at one time or another, and of course, come to regret it shortly thereafter.

To compound matters I missed a great window of opportunity for redemption when I got married. I know I should've gotten hitched to someone who abounded in cynicism, someone who could haggle, someone with the merciless business ethics of a hawk. We would've made a well-balanced team. Me floating dreamily along like a balloon on a string, tethered to reality by the firm hands of my pragmatic partner. Of course, I didn't do that.

No, I met another balloon. A really wonderful, pretty, funny balloon with a laugh like a summer breeze. A woman who would gladly give me everything I needed in this life—except the cynic gene. Mind you, I don't regret it for one moment.

Our home is full of laughter, love and joy. We are great together, but we are also a blank cheque waiting to be signed. We have all the business savvy of Mother Teresa. Luckily we have been blessed with a voluminous sense of humour. Our necks are constantly sore from all the looking back and laughing we do.

It's all funny in hindsight. The drunken chimney sweep who made off with our deposit, the bipolar furniture maker who threatened to ransom our harvest table and most recently the jolly, fat crook who swore up and down that the bush cord of wood he'd delivered was as dry as the Mojave. I might as well be burning frozen fish sticks in my wood stove. Freaking hilarious. But where is the karma?

I know, in my naive little heart of hearts, that love and trust should always be my first choices. I hope they always will be. I couldn't sleep at night if I lived my life any other way. But, all the same, wouldn't it be swell if, in this life, we acquired nice points? Points that could be cashed in at a moment's notice for instant karmic revenge? Kind of like a customer loyalty program for being trusting.

"Oh honey, those roofers did a horrible job. And they've left nails all over the yard!"

"That's OK sweetie, we have enough karma points to give the whole crew hives and still have enough left for the plumber's tumour. And just think, we can do it all over the phone!" How sweet would that be?

Some things are just really hard to get your head around—the hatred in the Middle East, slavery, the Holocaust…Madonna writing a children's book. This last one has me shaking my head. I suppose it is a testimony to the wondrous power for change that children can bring into one's life. Goodness knows I've experienced that, but I am still skeptical.

I'm also a little ticked. So Madonna rolls out of bed for five minutes and scribbles a few cutesy notes to her kid. Suddenly she's a children's author? Doesn't this kick a little literary sand in the faces of people like Roald Dahl, Maurice Sendak and even the great one, Dr. Seuss? I mean, these were writers who devoted a lifetime to honing their craft, to making sure they offered only the very best to children. It was not a hobby to them.

Of course, I could be wrong in my snobbish prejudgment of Madonna's efforts. Who knows what kinds of gems might come from the same rich vein that gave us such immortal ballads as "Papa Don't Preach," "Material Girl," and the deeply introspective "Vogue?"

Perhaps Sendak and Seuss would've enjoyed even greater success had they taken a page or two from Madonna's book. Might this be a better world today if, as children, we had been raised on such wonders as "Horton Busts a Rhyme," "One Fish, Two Fish, Hot Fish, Nude Fish" or "The Cat in the Bra?" It's hard to say.

What is perhaps more troubling is will Madonna's entry into the world of literature open the doors for other celebrity would-be authors? Try these on for size:

Thomas the Tanked Engine by Ralph Klein

Cars and Trucks and Things That Blow Up by Osama Bin Laden

Furious George and the Wacky Iraqis by George W. Bush

Dr. Do-Little by Jean Chretien

Charlie and the Chocolate Sweatshop by Kathie Lee Gifford

The Emperor's New Nose by Michael Jackson

The Borrowers by Winona Ryder

Hickory Dickory Glock by Robert Blake

Charlotte's Portfolio by Martha Stewart

The Jungle Bookie by Pete Rose

The Fight Before Christmas by Mike Tyson

As I say, I may be doing Madonna a grave injustice by not giving her the benefit of the doubt here. I'm quite sure she loves her child—as long as he doesn't wear her stuff. I just wonder about her talent and her motives. It's been a while since she had anything approaching a number one hit and she's dropped well out of the limelight, the stuff that is like oxygen to most celebrities. Why not reinvent herself as a writer then? How hard can it be?

Of course all of this begs the question, are there any writers out there who haven't published a bestseller in a while who might want to jump into the music scene? I wish Madonna luck and I'd like to think parenting has given her a dose or two of healthy reality that she was missing previously, but most of me remains unconvinced. Once a whack job always a whack job. I kind of like her music, but I'm no more interested in reading her books than I am in watching Norman Mailer strut across a stage in a metal push-up bra and headset bellowing "Like a Virgin."

Victory Over Cancer Best Kind of Party

My eight-year-old came home the other day, flushed with excitement. His class was going to have a party the next day. It was going to be a big deal. I mentally ran through all the usual suspects; it wasn't Halloween, Christmas was long gone, Valentine's too, and it wasn't Easter yet. What was left? He then explained to me the whole class was celebrating the fact one of the little girls in the class had just had her last chemotherapy treatment after a long and exhausting battle with leukemia. She was free and clear.

He skipped off happily, leaving me completely blown away. I loved him intensely for his naked enthusiasm about this party and his simple, childlike understanding of the reason for it and I loved his teacher for having it. The fact was not lost on me for a second that, had that little girl and her cancer been in my Grade 3 class, there would more than likely have been no party. Tragically, there would have been nothing to celebrate—just an empty desk.

When I was in Grade 3, leukemia and chemotherapy were not part of our lexicon. I don't remember if any of the kids in my class had cancer or any other life-threatening illnesses. I probably wouldn't have known if they had. I remember Timmy P. seemed to have a perpetually snotty nose, and I'm pretty sure Wayne M. was a little "tecched," but that was as far as it went.

People didn't talk about such things back then, certainly not in front of the children. It wasn't considered healthy. But here, now, in this little girl's class, the other kids had been aware of the illness from the get go. And, more importantly, they'd been a big part of the healing process too. I remember two years ago, when this same little girl was first diagnosed, going to the school to videotape her classmates so that she, in the hospital, could remain connected to them and her old life somehow.

I remember crowds of pudgy, grinning faces in my viewfinder waving and screaming out their jubilant "get wells." I remember the walls of those classrooms plastered with pictures of this little girl in her hospital room, her smiling, freckled face beaming out from under a goofy hat that covered her newly-bald head. I remember a community coming together to create a fund to help the little girl's family deal with new and crushing medical expenses, in stark contrast to the silent ignorance of my own Grade 3 world where no one knew. Now, we all knew. And I am convinced we were all better for it. The unexpected joy I felt upon hearing the reason for the little girl's party is proof enough of that statement.

I've thought about it for a while now and I kind of wish the whole town had been invited to that classroom party. I would've gone. It's important that we share the grief in this life, but it's just as important, I think, that we share the cake.

CHAIN-LETTER EMAILS JUST A WASTE OF VALUABLE TIME

At least once a month, sometimes more, I receive one of those sac-charine, cutesy chain-letter type emails. You know the ones where you have to scroll down one line at a time, no peeking! Then do something stupid at each line like "Think of a colour" or "Imagine what kind of animal you'd like to be" or "Pick a dead dictator" (OK, that was mine) until you finally come to the end where it is magically revealed, to your utter amazement, that you are a loving, hard-working person, who can get a little crazy sometimes, but who believes in people!

Wow you say, that is sooo true! This thing is sooo accurate! It's spooky! No, it's goofy. I get email with the subject line reading some-thing like "Try this, it's hilarious!" or "This is so fun!" or "This really works!" and I want to vomit. I know what's coming. But, of course, I still do it. My lurid fascination with the depths of human idiocy drives me to follow the damn thing, line for line, all the way down to its ri-diculous conclusion.

Where I draw the line however, is in the chain-type directions. "Pass this letter along to X number of people and you will experience good luck some time today! Don't break the chain! A friend of mine passed it along at noon and within 10 minutes she had lunch! Is that wild or what?" or "This is really serious. A guy I work with broke the chain and 20 years later he died!"

Be forewarned folks, I am a professional chain-letter breaker. I have personally broken more chains than anyone I know. I am responsible for that little girl in Honduras not getting the operation she needed. I am the reason those orphans in Nicaragua were shot. I am probably the reason you are not rich beyond your wildest dreams today. One of my greatest pleasures in life is hitting that little delete button. And guess what? Far from being destitute and unhappy, I am one of the luckiest people I know!

What happens to people to make them believe in this stuff? Here they sit with thousands of dollars worth of mind-boggling technology on their desk and all they can think to do with it is broadcast garbage mumbo-jumbo the intellectual level of the Dark Ages. Think I'm over-reacting? I wonder. After all, is "Send this along to 10 people and good things will happen to you," that much of a stretch from "Rub this toad on your forehead and you will not get the plague?"

The other ones I love are the messages with just enough credibility to hook millions. "XYZ Software Company is testing their new email debugging software! This is not a hoax! Send this letter to everyone in your address book and you will all receive a check for a billion dollars from its founder. This is totally on the level. A friend of mine who knows a guy who cleans the crappers there verified it for me. Just don't break the chain or that little girl in Honduras is as good as dead."

Sorry. Click. Scratch one Honduran cutie. Send me bad jokes by the bucketful, send me cheesy thoughts of the day, send me rhymes with the word Nantucket in them if you feel so moved. But please, *please* don't send me this stuff.

THE BATTLE LINES ARE DRAWN

I'm a little horrified to admit I've become a war junkie. I keep drifting back to the TV set for my hits of CNN. I know it's not good for me. All it does is raise my blood pressure and lower my hope for the future, but I can't help it. I've tried to wean myself away by taking the war in smaller doses—on the radio or in the newspapers. It's no good. I need my imbedded reports, my snazzy "Patton-esque" intro music, my grainy sound bites delivered by moist-lipped, perfectly-coiffed presenters. I am pathetic.

But, I think I've figured out, finally, why I am so compelled to watch. Goodness knows it's not for the content, for what actually passes for real, hard news in a 24-hour period over that network might fill a specimen cup. No, it's because when I watch, when I let it all engage me totally, I am suddenly and painfully aware of all the maddening dichotomies within me. The war has become a mirror for me that I cannot stop myself from gazing into. Maybe you've experienced the same thing.

On one day I am shown Neil the pacifist, the peace lover who opposes war of any kind and who genuinely grieves for the death of any human. On the next, or even later in that same day, I come face to face with Neil the screaming, angry redneck who wants to grab an M-16 and personally take out Saddam and his prehistoric cadre. It's astounding. How can these two people exist in the same body?

I think my problem may lie in the fact I am a black and white thinker in a world of greys and halftones. To me, the instructions for living have always been very simple. We share our toys, we ask nicely, and we don't hit. How difficult is that to grasp? How can anybody not comprehend that?

Unfortunately, such monochromatic thinking does not leave room for the Saddams and the Adolphs and the Moammars of the world. For whatever reasons, they don't play by the same rules.

They just don't get it. And it makes me so mad I could just—kill them? Holy hypocrisy, Batman! Now what? To muddy the waters even more, I know very well the good guys in this war haven't always been that good. You see the fix I'm in?

Sometimes I think the answer must lie in siding with honour and righteousness. After all, how can that be wrong? But those two are slippery little creatures. Just when you think you've found them, and understand them, they change clothes, or flags or religions. More halftones.

And every minute I am in this muddle, someone, Iraqi or American, Christian or Muslim—someone with dreams and hopes and friends who will cry for weeks when they are gone, is in very real danger of dying. Pretty freaking high stakes, huh?

But I'll let you in on a dirty little secret I've discovered about myself lately. I'm not proud of it, but I can't deny it either. Sometimes, I just don't care.

Anybody else been there? Man, growing up is hard to do. Where's Neil Sedaka when you need him?

Just How Would You Spend Your Last Hours on Earth?

Is it just me or are things getting a little biblical lately? We've got a war raging in the birthplace of civilization (coincidence, I think not), we've got famine in, well, let's face it, we've always had famine, and now we have SARS breathing down our necks like a modern-day plague. All we need is a little pestilence and the four horsemen of the apocalypse are saddled up, baby. In fact we might already have pestilence. I just don't know what the heck pestilence is. I think it has something to do with expired dairy products.

As I write these words, in April no less, it is snowing so heavily I cannot see the house across the street. A house, mind you, with the street number 27, which, while not necessarily the mark of Satan, might well be the mark of say, Satan's Uncle Murray. Who knows? Signs and portents my friends, signs and portents.

Surely you must have noticed them too. Those strange little occurrences or phenomena that give one pause and make your hair stand on end; a teenager walking past makes eye contact and says hello to you. A stranger lets his dog poop on your lawn and then he cleans up after the dog. The people at 407 ETR send you a bill—and it's accurate. And perhaps the most chilling sign of the end of times, the Leafs are winning. Eerie isn't it?

What would we do if it all came to an end? How would you spend the last hours on earth? That's a tough one. Of course, many would want to be with their loved ones. Others may wish to be with their wives or husbands. Still others might want to throw caution to the wind and do those things they've always wanted to but never dared: hang-gliding, mountain climbing, fudging a GST return. And many no doubt, will seek solace in the good book, finding their "piece" in the swimsuit edition.

Of course there are the children to think of too. How to spare the little ones the anguish of Armageddon? I really think the answer lies in video games. After all, during the kind of catatonia most kids drift into while playing those damn things, you could set a bomb off and they wouldn't know it.

Their brain, entering a kind of video survival mode, pares its activity down to only the most essential functions, shunting most of the body's blood flow to the fingers and thumbs. If video companies included a saline drip and a diaper with their games, kids would never leave the television.

Personally, I'm not sure how I would spend those last moments. There's still so much I want to experience—learning to paint, playing a sonata on the piano, belching the alphabet. Then again, I may well end up helping those less fortunate than myself—volunteering in a homeless shelter or hospice or maybe just sitting with the elderly and comforting them simply by my presence. Right. Who's kidding whom? When they drop the big one I'll be knee deep in the world's biggest banana split, pal. If I'm going out, I'm going out lactose-intolerant.

Squealers Unite!
You Too Can Tell Tales

When was the last time you told on somebody? I personally can't remember. Weird when you consider that telling on somebody was, for years, the number one weapon in any kid's arsenal. It was the ace in the hole, the trump card, the smart bomb of payback. I guess at some point in a kid's life, telling on people becomes frowned upon. Suddenly you're no longer a helpless victim or innocent witness, you are simply a tattler or worse still—a rat, a stoolie or a fink. Too bad. There's a heck of a lot of power in those two little words, "I'm telling." There are times in the life of an adult when they might come in very handy.

What if, for instance, upon delivery of your new sofa you notice the delivery guys have tracked mud all over your carpet? Instead of taking up precious moments of your life trying to diplomatically bring the faux pas to their attention, wouldn't it be ever so much more effective, not to mention fun, to simply point an accusing finger at the mud and utter a breathless "I'm telling!" It's the open ended-ness of the threat that makes it so perfect. Telling who? Telling what? In the face of such an all-encompassing hex, service people would be falling over themselves to right the wrong. We are all hard-wired to panic at the mere mention of those words.

Another more devious use of tattling might be during the hated automobile purchase negotiations. How many times have you felt obliged to some slippery salesman who gives you the old "Look, don't tell my manager, I mean I'm probably gonna get fired for doing this, but I'll let you have the leather and the air for just $500 extra."

It's at this point, expert hagglers tell us, that we are to get up and silently walk to the door. It's supposed to rattle salespeople. But what if you got up, calmly stated, "I'm telling" and started walking towards the manager's door? Forget the moon roof and the alloy rims pal, you'll be talking loaded and 0% financing in no time.

Of course one has to be careful. There is, after all, a fine line between tattling and blackmail. One is an immature, knee-jerk reaction to being wronged—the other is a felony. You also have to pick your moments. Just as when you were a child you always ran the risk of getting pounded when you threatened to snitch on someone, the same risk is inherent as an adult. While an anonymous phone call to Crime Stoppers is a positive and generally safe use of tattling, I don't think when a buddy confides, over a beer or two, that he has been fooling around on his wife, "I'm telling" is an appropriate response. It occurs to me, now that I think about it, that telling on people is probably practised more than I had first thought. In fact, our society holds finking in such high esteem that we have created a special place for adult tattletales. It's called the Witness Protection Program.

WHAT'S YOUR PASSWORD—I FORGET

I'm developing a serious case of password burnout. I suppose it's the price one pays for all the technological advancement and conveniences we enjoy, but it's starting to drive me a little ape. How many times throughout my day am I prompted for a password or a secret code or an entry number? In other words, how many times a day is my integrity and honesty challenged? Am I really who I say I am? So prove it—give me the password.

I understand these things are there for my own protection. I am glad my ATM card requires a PIN. Likewise I'm happy to know not just anyone can use my credit card online. Good thing too. I love buying stuff over the Internet. I am the guy all those websites love to see coming. Part of it is the fact I live in the country, some distance from major shopping areas, but mainly it's because I just think it's so cool that, with a couple of clicks of a mouse, stuff gets delivered right to my house! And they have things on the Internet that you just can't get anywhere else. Try and find a real store that sells budgie socks or a solar-powered couch.

But I digress—badly. My point is, while I appreciate the need for security, I am not a security-minded individual. I cannot tell you how many times I have had to hit that little "Forgot Your Password?" button. I tend to daydream a lot, it's part and parcel of what I do for a living. I also try very hard to live my life in the present moment. Unfortunately that means that large chunks of the past sometimes get bulk-erased. It's who I am. I'm not at all ashamed of it, you understand, but there are some days when I could really use a "Forgot Your Name?" button.

Some places, no doubt, in an effort to deal with annoying people like me, have built-in safety devices to prompt you into remembering your secret codes and passwords. They may ask you for your mother's maiden name or the name of a special place such as, "Where were you married?"

This would be very helpful were it not for my penchant for being particularly arcane when setting these things up. In my paranoia I always feel that anyone, with a modicum of digging, could discover things as mundane as my mother's maiden name or where I was married. And so, I cleverly outfox any would-be trespasser—and subsequently myself—by setting up the most ridiculously convoluted questions imaginable. Never does it occur to me at the time, of course, that I might, several months or even weeks later, have a little difficulty remembering the first place I saw a bird or my mother's platelet count or the number of Confederate dead at Gettysburg. As a result I spend an inordinate amount of time on the phone with tech support.

I think from now on, when they first ask me to create a password I will type in the words, "I forget," What a great password. I'd never be stumped again.

"What's your password?"

"I forget."

"Come on in, Mr. Crone".

We seem to be in the middle of movie sequel hell right now. Take a quick glance through the entertainment section of any newspaper and you'll see what I mean. Everything old is new again. The interesting thing is that this recycling of themes seems to limit itself largely to the cinema only.

Occasionally you'll see a hit TV show spawn a spinoff or two, but these are not technically sequels. The phenomenon almost never happens in the world of print.

Some authors have made good livings deliberately cranking out books starring the same character, but these—with the exception perhaps of the fantastically successful *Harry Potter* series—are usually niche kind of books, not blockbusters. The big books, the ones everyone has heard about, the ones we re-read again and again and study in school are somehow sacrosanct.

Why, for instance has no one ever penned a sequel to Melville's classic *Moby Dick?* Surely there is an audience out there for the much sexier *Moby 2—A View to a Krill* or *Dive Hard*. Where is *Uncle Tom's Cabin Cruiser? The Manchurian Incumbent? Atlas Yawned?* or *Hey Look, It's Godot?* And who wouldn't want to read more about F. Scott Fitzgerald's now middle-aged and somewhat pear-shaped protagonist in *The Great Fatsby?*

Aren't there also millions to be made in the very lucrative world of children's sequels? *The Cat in the Wheelchair? Where the Wild Things Were?* or the unsurprising but still very readable *There's Waldo?*

Don't forget, too, about that other clever plot-regurgitating device, the prequel. The *Star Wars* people have very adeptly mined millions from our pockets using this little invention so who knows how many copies *The Second Last of the Mohicans* might have sold? Or what about *To Take Aim at a Mockingbird?* or *Gulliver's Itinerary?*

Does all this sound silly? Laughable? Why then will we line up in droves to see endless variations and permutations of *Rockys*, *Predators* and *Terminators*? I'm not pointing fingers here, folks. I'll be in those lineups with you. I'm currently looking forward tremendously to hearing Arnie say his newest five lines of dialogue as only he can.

My question is, why is it only the movies? I love books, probably even more than I love films. But I really don't think I would be at all interested in reading a sequel to any of my favourites.

Perhaps that's because a really good story, a story that resonates with something deep down inside you, whether told in print or on celluloid, leaves nothing else to be said. It is the complete package and anything else is merely chaff.

Or maybe—and more to the point—it's probably something much more mundane. Maybe publishers just haven't gotten as hungry for our money as film producers have.

If that is indeed the case, then it won't be long at all before bookstore displays are crammed with the likes of *Catch-23, 1985, Funeral of a Salesman,* and *Still Quiet on the Western Front.*

A Dirty Job but It's Gotta Be Done

On the back of my shampoo bottle, down at the bottom, it says "Questions? Call 1-800-555-5555." Who calls that number? And more importantly, why? What kind of desperate shampoo conundrum are people getting themselves into that they need to call that number? What kind of questions could you possibly need to ask? It's a bottle of shampoo, not a particle accelerator.

But, of course, we are talking about human beings after all and, as we all know, there is no limit to both our genius and our stupidity.

"Hi, shampoo hotline? Listen, are we supposed to wash the hairs one at a time or can we do 'em all in a big bunch?"

"Hello, shampoo guy? Yeah, I'm in a bit of a pickle. I was working the lather into my eyelashes, 'cause they're hair aren't they? And now it kinda burns. Also, I can't see so good."

"Help me please! I must've left it on my head for too long. I think it leached into my brain, 'cause now I can't think of nothing dirty."

"Hi there…I was ah, washing my hair and I dropped the bottle, then when I bent over to pick it up I slipped and fell and ah…landed on the ah…well you're gonna laugh when you hear this…"

I'll bet you that 1-800 number is ringing off the hook 24/7.

The scary thing is, on items that should have a "Questions? Call 1-800-etc." number, items like chainsaws, bear traps or firearms, items that can kill you, we find nothing at all. I think it would show uncommon good sense to have emblazoned across the stalk of a rifle the words "Questions? Please, for the love of Pete, put this thing down and call 1-800-etc." But no, those words of wisdom are sagely reserved for the real dangers—the shampoo, the toothpaste and the hemorrhoid cream.

Makes you wonder what kind of person they've got on the other end of that 1-800 number, doesn't it? I picture some balding, chain-smoking guy, one hand nervously gripping a microphone, the other loosening his tie. Sort of like a harried air traffic controller for shampoo near misses.

"All right, let's start with your name?" he says in a firm, yet friendly voice.

"Vivian," comes the timid, frightened reply.

"That's a pretty name Vivian. Now, listen to me. I'm gonna get you out of that shower safely, you understand. Everything's gonna be just fine, as long as you do what I tell you."

"OK."

"Good girl. Now, in front of you, Vivian, you should see two knobs, one is for hot, the other is cold. Can you see them, Vivian?"

"Uh-huh."

"That's my girl. Now I want you to slowly turn the knob on the left clockwise. Can you do that for me Viv?"

"I'll try…Oww, it burns, it burns!"

"Dammit Vivian! Clockwise! I said clockwise! Get your nose up! You're too low Vivian! You're overshooting the bath mat!"

Yes, I imagine it's a difficult life being a shampoo crisis worker. For every five or six you get safely rinsed and towelled off, there's one that, despite all your efforts, just goes down the drain. Try living with that on your conscience.

It's Only Rock 'n Roll, but I Don't Like It

As I write these words, D-Day, or Downsview Day, is only one week away. As you read them, it will be upon us.

Let me be clear at the outset of this piece that I am not currently a big Rolling Stones fan. I didn't even really care for them when they still vaguely resembled human beings. I am even less of a fan of paying through the nose for a ticket and taking out a second mortgage on my house for parking so I can then walk for two hours to stand in the middle of 800 acres of sun-scorched scrub grass and bubbling hot tarmac, shoulder to sweat-soaked shoulder with 450,000 screaming, two-legged rock lemmings.

Suffice it to say, I would rather stick pins through my eyes than be within a 50-mile radius of the place on July 30. (Which coincidentally is roughly where you'll find the first available parking spots for the event.)

I don't think the promoters and organizers are really getting it. So far they've been basing most of their contingency plans for this thing on the set-up for last year's very successful (unless you own an Idomo store) World Youth Day. You may remember the fiasco involving tons of human port-a-potty waste that turned the day into more of a poop visit than Pope visit for one bearded Scandinavian retailer. The numbers of bodies attending both events are about the same but that's where the parallel comes to an abrupt and very ugly halt.

Has it occurred to no one that these are not bright-eyed, freshly scrubbed peace pilgrims but hard-core Stones, AC/DC and Rush devotees? I don't know how much dope, booze and beer those pilgrims put away, but I'll bet you it's nothing compared to what real rock 'n rollers can consume. And yes, I've heard how stringent security is going to be, but you and I both know that when it comes to sneaking in contraband, rock fans are more inventive than the French Underground. Personally, I'm calling my broker and telling him to sell everything and buy as much Doritos stock as he can get his hands on between now and July 30.

I also seriously doubt there were more than a handful of frantic female Pope groupies tearing their tops off when the pontiff arrived on stage. But you watch what happens when Mick starts strutting and pouting. Not to mention when AC/DC gets it cranked up. That's going to be the mother of all mosh pits, my friend, and unless you're into group prostate exams, I wouldn't go anywhere near it.

I suppose this monstrosity's heart is in the right place. All of the profits are, ostensibly, going to fight SARS and to help out Toronto's problem-plagued tourist industry. But I still can't help but feel it's a nightmare waiting to happen.

Then again, maybe it is just me. I am, after all, the guy who breaks into a sweat if the checkout line at the grocery store gets too long. Might do me a world of good to take my top off and flash Mick and the boys. I just don't know how long Suzanne could keep me up on her shoulders.

My two boys and I just got back from our semi-annual pilgrimage to a Canadian amusement park. Once again we had a ball rattling our brains around inside our heads doing loop-de-loops at 90 km/hr and once again, to my utter sadness and disappointment, it looked like we were surrounded by the cast of *Chained Heat*.

The only difference this year was that I noticed my 11-year-old staring at the nearly naked teenage girls. My eight-year-old either hasn't cottoned to the allure of the female form yet or he was just better at hiding it than we were. I suspect the latter.

I'm not exaggerating when I tell you how much these experiences disturb me. I find it absolutely spirit-crushing to see everywhere around me young women whose meager self-esteem clings anemically to a pair of half-exposed breasts or a suggestively waving tattooed rump. Never mind what's inside baby, get a load of this wrapping paper!

To be fair, the young men are no better. So many of them wrapped up in navel gazing, doing their damnedest to look hard and tough and utterly detached in their chains and headbands, swearing and spitting and waving their hands around like a pathetic bunch of carpal tunnel victims.

I don't mean to sound like some myopic, right wing, brush cut hankering for the good ol' days. I consider myself a fairly enlightened individual. I read Whitman, Thoreau, Emerson as well as *Maxim*. I also remember that the good ol' days weren't always that good. We have always had apples who, for a myriad of reasons, went bad. We always will. What I suppose I am lamenting here is the large-scale abandonment of parental responsibility I see around me.

Who is helping these kids? Listen people, let your sons and daughters express themselves on the outside as they will and must, but for goodness' sake make sure you have shown them what lies inside first. Show them their iron, show them their art, show them their infinite potential. Teach them that they are born unique and wonderful and that nothing Calvin Klein or Britney Spears or Kobe Bryant says or does can change that. And first and foremost, let's let them be children for as long as it takes. What some people expose their young kids to, out of nothing more than apathy, is absolutely criminal.

We are flushing a generation of wonder down the crapper folks—because we are lazy parents. Parenting is a voluntary activity. You signed on for it so suck it up. Stand for something. Raise the bar. Money talks very loudly. So, tell the manufacturers of television shows, films, commercials, music, fashion—anything that affects your precious child—just exactly what you think of what they're doing.

Use your power and make informed, smart choices. Things will change in a big hurry. I'm no book burner. I will always be first in line in support of individual rights and freedoms. Understand, however, that included in there is my children's right to their childhood and a bright and happy future. I'll go down swinging protecting that.

Big Gladys Had Big Plans for my Pictures

Very occasionally I get fan mail. Not from Canadians, mind you. Canadians, you may remember, do not watch Canadian TV shows. I know. I'm Canadian and I don't.

No, most of my fan mail, believe it or not, comes from Europe. Apparently I can't walk down the street in Upper Liechtenstein without getting mobbed and I'm huge in Mermansk. I did have one groupie from the Maritimes for a short while. She sent me tins of moose meat. No lingerie, no suggestive polaroids, no perfumed propositions— moose meat. Go figure.

Recently though, I think I hit a new low. I received a fan letter from the Arizona State Penitentiary. My fan (in the interests of privacy we'll just call him Big Gladys) referred to me as a big star, a huge celebrity and extremely talented. Apparently they don't watch Canadian TV in Arizona either.

It didn't take me long to realize that Big Gladys had no idea who I was, nor did he really care. He had gotten my name off an Internet celebrity list and was hitting me up for as many autographed pictures as he could lay his bloodstained hands on. These, in turn, he would sell for 20 cents a copy to any interested cons, using the profits for such prison necessities as smokes, drugs or, if he were really frugal, perhaps acquiring a small Latino cell mate.

To Big Gladys's credit, he as much as told me so. This was a scam to earn him a little mad money. I might actually have sent him a few pictures had he not tried to con me further into thinking that he was really doing this to try and turn his life around—20 cents at a time. You see, he also happened to mention, just in passing, that he was only two years into a 65-year sentence. Sixty-five years. You have to have done something particularly monstrous to get 65 years, even in Arizona. (I think President Bush's old stomping grounds, Texas, is the only place you can still get 65 years for a parking infraction. It's the death penalty if you run a meter out and you happen to be black.)

Anyway, I figured Big Gladys probably knew his way around a wood chipper pretty well, if you get my drift.

Also, you had to figure if a peanut brain like Big Gladys was into this scam, then probably every other con in the joint was hip to it too. They'd be swapping celebrity photographs around in there like hockey cards. And if Robert DeNiro or Al Pacino were the equivalent of a Phil Esposito or Wayne Gretzky, then I'm sure I'd pretty much be the Eric Nesterenko of celebrity photos. I'd wind up in the spokes of the prison exercise bike going "clack, clack, clack, clack" like a motorcycle engine. I'm not sure if my ego could take that.

Needless to say I didn't send him any photographs, signed or otherwise. Maybe I'll send him some of that moose meat. That stuff doesn't go bad, does it?

Funny how sometimes we see more of our real self when there is no light. Many of us looked into the darkness of our souls during the blackout—and many of us did not like what we saw.

It is dusk on Thursday evening. The first night without power, the first night of total darkness. The shadows creep up on my little town, somehow blacker and more ominous without the sentinel hum of electricity through the wires overhead. I am alone. Suzanne and the boys are away at my parents' cottage—a blessing.

The house seems cavernous and lonely and so I opt to go out and walk around. After a moment or two I notice for the first time in years the voices in my head are silent. No more frantic "They're all staring at you!" or "Your fly's undone! Your fly's undone!" or 'Those pants make you look fat you know." I make a mental note to get a thorough MRI when the power comes back—*if* the power comes back. Yes, that's the real question isn't it? The one none of us wants to ask ourselves on this night of questions.

Main Street is cloaked in an inky, dangerous darkness when I arrive. The looting and pillaging has already begun. Normally decent, law-abiding citizens have somehow, with the advancing blackness, become greedy, bug-eyed monsters. Here a man emerges from a broken storefront window clutching a tub of ice cream under each arm. There two elderly women have smashed in the glass of the beauty parlour and sit illegally under hair dryers. Down the street rival gangs of farm thugs battle viciously for the rights to a stolen manure spreader. The dark underbelly of a small town.

I decide I had better get home and I arrive not a minute too soon. A pack of wild-eyed Lion's Club members-gone-bad are roving up and down my street bullying people into wearing purple vests. I slip into my house through the back and lock the doors. Peering cautiously through the front curtains I notice the pack of Lions has now swelled to nearly twice its original size, having been joined by a sneering gaggle of Daughters of the Eastern Star. The women heckle passersby as they defiantly wave quilts with all manner of profanity delicately stitched into them over their heads. That can only be bad. I slowly close the curtains.

And now I am alone. Truly alone. I get into bed, fully dressed and although the night is asphyxiatingly hot and humid I pull the comforter up around me. Slowly, thankfully, against the horrible backdrop of the Masons setting fire to the post office, I fall asleep.

Sometime later I awaken to horrible screaming. Sitting bolt upright in bed I realize with relief it is only the radio playing a Yoko Ono song. The power is back on. The sun is up, the birds are singing. And look, through my bedroom window I see a group of Lions in purple vests picking up litter.

I slump back against my pillow with a smile on my face. Yes, I think, we have our dark side, but this is still a pretty nice little town.

Fall Fair Offers a Chance for a World of Discovery

Each year at the Fall Fair I learn a little more about my town. I pick up stuff about people and even myself which couldn't possibly be learned anywhere else. For instance, I now know Marge W. gets really huffy if you touch her butter tarts. Elmay G. snaps the arms off the competitors' gingerbread men when she thinks no one is looking and Roy M. always sneaks a gourd into the fair that looks vaguely sexual.

I learn there will always be a generous crowd of young boys watching whenever the oldest Hemplethwaite girl wears a tube top on any ride that spins. I discover the most romantic spot in town is at the top of the Ferris wheel at dusk. I slip the carnie operating it an extra fiver to keep my wife and me up there for a few extra moments.

I see that the brat down the street is remarkably proficient at target shooting. I make a mental note to smile at him more from now on. I vow not to play bingo anywhere near Kay L. or any of her blue-haired gang. They are dangerous women who carry their dabbers in holsters. They would eat my lunch.

I figure out how to lean on a tractor wheel and tilt my baseball hat just so when I talk to old farmers—who just happen to be about the most interesting guys on earth. I deduce why Velma T. really is the queen of lemon meringue and I now know why Vic and Carl cannot keep their hands off Doris's cream puffs.

I learn to give any child with a soft ice cream cone a wide berth. I understand that if a child says he's going to pee his pants on a ride, he may well be telling the truth. I find out the Melderson boy has a hair trigger epiglottis. I determine that six feet is not always a safe distance from someone who is throwing up.

I get the idea horses may be smarter than all of the rest of us. I realize the demolition derby is way more fun when you sit with female truckers. I glean that it's best not to stare at female truckers' tattoos. I cover my kids' ears when the female truckers catch me staring at their tattoos.

I discover you can probably die if you eat candy floss really quickly and then chug a cola. And I find that, no matter what flavour, after the first pound, fudge doesn't taste so good.

I find out there is no nicer smell in the world than french fries, cotton candy and horse manure carried along on a crisp fall breeze.

I see what seems like an outrageous ticket price is actually some of the best money I will ever spend; I am buying memories for my children and me.

Finally, as I walk home that night, amidst the giggles and yawns and murmured conversations of my neighbours and their families, I learn why I live where I live. These are good people.

The Children's Allowance Plan—
Spend as I Say, Not as I Do

After much discussion, we have decided to try an allowance system in our house. In exchange for performing certain menial duties and helping out around the house, the boys will be rewarded with a sum of money at the end of each week.

I am not certain I am comfortable with this set-up. I never received an allowance as a kid. In my house it was expected that, because we were part of a family, we would chip in and do our part to help out without any thought of being paid for it. And it's not like we went without anything. If we needed money for some little thing all we had to do was ask. My parents were always more than happy to tell us "No."

I'll admit I was always a little envious of those kids who did get an allowance, kids who had money for candy and bubble gum, kids who actually went into the variety store to buy stuff, not just to stare at the nudie magazines. But I got over it. I actually went on to lead a fairly successful, happy life in spite of my non-allowanced youth. And today, when I go into the variety store, I buy stuff *and* I look at the nudie magazines.

But my wife, who is a lovely woman and who could probably take me in three out of four falls, assures me that if the allowance is monitored properly, the children will gain valuable knowledge in the handling of money. It will be knowledge that will stand them in good stead as financially responsible adults. That's a phrase that is, coincidentally, completely foreign to both her and me. Suzanne and I have all the financial smarts of a pair of magpies. If it's shiny and new we must have it. While our impulsive lifestyle has undoubtedly kept things fresh and fun, and certainly exciting for our bank manager, there is no question it could stand to be tempered with at least a little monetary acumen.

Which leads me to the only real loophole in this closely monitored allowance plan. How am I, a fiscally challenged adult, supposed to be relied upon to make sure my kids handle their money properly? It's a little like leaving the fox to guard the henhouse, isn't it?

"Well boys, you've each got a crisp, new five dollar bill in your hands. Now, we could safely tuck that money away in a boring old GIC earning a paltry 2.5% or we could buy ourselves a pant load of sponge toffee! Girls dig a guy with a bag full of sponge toffee, ya know! Or hey, look! If we put all that money together we can buy a new transforming action figure. This one's totally amazing. When he's not battling evil he turns into a humidifier! How cool is that?"

You see what I mean? It doesn't really bode well. I need someone to monitor me. Anybody want a job? I'll give you an allowance!

Homework's Nothing But Drudgery

I can't believe the amount of stuff my kids carry on their backs as they head off to school. You'd think they were trekking into deepest, darkest jungles or something. All that's missing is a machete and a compass.

Each morning, their mother and I have to help them into their backpacks, one of us steadying the kids, the other hefting the huge weight onto their little shoulders. They can barely walk under all that tonnage. I haven't looked, but I wouldn't be surprised if the route to school were strewn with dozens of struggling kids, turned turtle under the weight of those darn packs.

In the winter it's worse. The boys stumble out the door looking like Sherpas at a K2 base camp.

When did all this start? As a kid, the most I can remember carrying to school was a grudge, or maybe a macaroni or toothpick sculpture. In the wintertime my hands were almost always full, of course—but they were full of snowballs. We didn't need backpacks crammed with binders and textbooks and indoor shoes.

That's something else that makes me crazy—the indoor shoes concept. I must've been asleep at the switch when they rammed that little rule through. Now parents, who can barely keep their kids in shoes at the best of times, have to shell out twice the coin for a pair of shoes the kid will wear half as much. What's next? Indoor pants?

I'd really like to know what happened to change things. When I was in public school, my desk was where I kept all my stuff. It stayed in there. Very occasionally, I might have to bring home a spelling book or something from the library, but it was invariably something I could carry in one hand. I didn't have to portage anything for crying out loud.

A big part of the problem is that kids these days get a lot more homework—something I think is ridiculous and unnecessary too. Homework is for kids who messed up during class. If you're dopey enough to waste your class time talking and annoying other children who are working, then you get to finish up at home while you listen to the kids who completed their class work playing ball and riding their bikes. Where's the incentive to work hard at school if you know you're just going to get plastered with take-home stuff anyway?

"OK kids, it's three o'clock, time to head home. Now be sure to complete pages seven through nine in your math books and read chapters 13 and 15 in your geography texts tonight."

"Why?"

"Ummm…just because."

I don't get it. You'll never convince me that adding on homework simply because the government said so makes people smarter or better learners. It just makes them tired. And it may end up creating a generation of adults with back problems.

Some people would have you think that kids today need more homework because they're shiftless and lazy. I think it's something simpler than that. I think they end up with homework because they're wasting precious class time putting on and taking off their indoor shoes.

There is a contest unfolding right now where all of us are invited to mail in our vote for the all-time greatest Canadian. It's an interesting exercise on many levels. For a couple of reasons I think most of us will have a hard time deciding. Firstly, unlike our banner-waving southern neighbours, we don't like to toot our own horn. As a nation, we are notoriously self-effacing. Secondly, if you ask 10 different Canadians you're likely to get 10 different answers. We are an independent and varied lot. It's part of our charm.

I have my own list of course, and while some of my choices may seem a bit curious, I have a hunch there may be some resonance here for you. Before I begin though, let me just make vividly clear that one individual whose name I have heard mentioned incessantly in regard to this contest will most certainly *not* be on my list—Wayne Gretzky.

"What?" I hear, amidst the gnashing of teeth and renting of jerseys. "The Great One? How can you possibly malign the Great One?" News flash folks; Wayne loves Canada so much, he lives in the U.S. I certainly can't fault him for leaving Edmonton, who wouldn't? But leaving Canada, in my books, is grounds for automatic disqualification. And coming back once a year to film a cheesy automobile commercial doesn't cut it. Frank Mahovlich didn't leave Canada, Wayner, and we made him a senator.

Now then, to the nominees. My number one choice has to be the guy who first thought to combine french fries, cheese curds and gravy. Not only is poutine a uniquely Canadian dish (you can get french fries, cheese curds and gravy together in the States, but it's almost always by accident), but it is absolutely jam-packed with really good things— really. Things like cheese curds and gravy and french fries. I don't have any hard data on this but I'm pretty sure poutine has saved at least as many lives as the influenza vaccine. And even the people who died eating it, died happy.

My second nominee is someone who has changed the lives of virtually everyone who has lived through a Canadian winter. I've no idea who they were but I think all Canucks owe a huge debt to the first idiots to slide recklessly down a snow-covered slope on a few curved pieces of wood and in the midst of such madness coin the now-famous term *toboggan* (which I believe is Ojibway for "Tree! For cryin' out loud Lou, there's a tree!")

Finally, I don't think any list of great Canadians would be complete without the following entry. Due in large part to the heroic actions of this one courageous and wise individual, countless Canadians no longer have to live in nightly agony and embarrassment. I'm talking, of course, about the Global Television executive who cancelled *Train 48*. Thank you from all of us.

CHRISTMAS TRADITIONS DIE HARD

This will be the first Christmas without letters to Santa. Both of my guys, now 10 and 13, are hip to what is really going on. I suspect they have been for some time, but they are, as I hope they always will be, somewhat reluctant to let go of the delightful fib.

So, I don't know if there will be letters to Santa this year. If there are, I will, more than likely, have to edit them. My oldest has become a bit of a 13-year-old Oscar Wilde and I'm not sure Santa would appreciate the full extent of his wit.

It's hard to watch them let go of this thing. I know that it was inevitable—and probably necessary—but it's still difficult. There are some milestones that, as a parent, you are thrilled to see your children pass: diapers, toilet-training, hickeys (hopefully in that order). All are important litmus tests that tell you your kid is functioning properly and on the right path; that you haven't screwed them up too badly—yet.

But the Santa Claus thing seems to run deeper than all those. Rooted in the belief in Santa Claus is the enormous power of magic, love and altruism. I can't think of any gifts I would rather give my children.

So we watch and we hope, although the facade has become tattered or perhaps come down entirely, that the point—the lesson—has remained and hit home.

This morning at breakfast, when we had this discussion, I saw that lost look of regret in my sons' eyes. I told them, though, that as much fun as it is to wait for Santa, it is far more satisfying to actually be Santa. I told them that as precious and enduring as my childhood memories of

Christmas are (and they are golden) my most memorable Christmases are the ones I have enjoyed as a parent. I told them that they have that to yet look forward to—that the more you really know and understand about Christmas and what is really going on, the better it gets.

So there may not be letters to Santa anymore. And I'm OK with that. The letter to Santa is, after all, all about me. What Santa can do for me, what Santa can bring me. This year, I've noticed, with some delight, that for the first time ever, my kids are excitedly asking about what they can do for others: "What would Mom like for Christmas?" "What would their brother like for Christmas?" And, dare I say it, "What would Dad like for Christmas?"

Something just as important—maybe *more* important than diapers and toilet training is taking place. Their worlds are expanding and their hearts are getting bigger. Yes, a little part of me laments the end of those beautifully scribbled notes left by the fireplace on Christmas Eve, but a far larger space is filled with pride at what good people they are becoming. I'm very happy about all this. I only hope I handle the hickey thing as well.

GIVE ME GADGETS OVER GIDGET ANY DAY

I can't help myself. I've become a gadget freak. I can happily spend hours flipping through pages and pages in a catalogue of the most useless electronic toys on the planet. My eyes begin to glaze over and I smile and nod my head knowingly as I think how much better my life would be if I had one of those flashlights that doubles as a hammer. I can't tell you how many times I've ruined a project by building it in the dark.

I burble happily just imagining how cool it would be to have a power tie rack in my closet. Never mind that I only have four ties in my possession. If I had that power tie rack, I would get more ties. Life would be better on so many levels. And if I got the one with the remote, I could actually lie in bed and rotate my ties. Think of the time saved. That's like, five minutes a day, multiplied by 365 days a year—wow, that's over 30 hours a year spent uselessly standing up and sorting through ties. That's more than a whole day that I would now be able to devote to other, more important things, like helping the needy, reading to impoverished inner-city youths or watching TV. Incredible.

But that's only the beginning. I gasp audibly as I come to the page with the turbo nose-hair trimmer.

How many times have you wished your nose hair trimmer had more horsepower? Man, there is nothing more frustrating than having some wimpy standard power nose hair trimmer get bogged down and twisted up in all that nose hair. But a turbo nose hair trimmer! That'd be different. That's the great thing about the word "turbo." You put that word in front of anything and it just gets better; turbo fridge, turbo cake, turbo wife. Just imagine.

And my gadget gazing isn't always only about me either. I'm always on the lookout for ways to make my wife's days easier as well. Like what about the misting pore cleanser with deep, penetrating suction? I'm not exactly clear on what that is, but you've got to admit it sounds pretty interesting. Or what about a fabulous home electrolysis system? My wife, thank goodness, doesn't have electrolysis yet, but as she gets older, who knows? Do I want to spend our golden years watching my bed-ridden wife waste away from electrolysis? Better safe than sorry, I say. And this isn't just an electrolysis set—it's a whole system.

System is another one of those words like turbo. It dresses up any-thing—*the Neil Crone vacuuming system, the Neil Crone eating system, the Neil Crone love-making system.* See? Give me a system and, sud-denly, I'm the go-to guy.

You can't get this kind of useful information just anywhere. You've got to look in a catalogue.

Time Alone Brings Understanding

My father-in-law died two weeks before Christmas, and, to tell you the truth, I'm still a little surprised at how much I miss him. We didn't get off to a really great start, he and I.

I'll never forget the night, many moons ago, when I called him to ask his permission to marry Suzanne. Smug little jerk that I was, I figured it was a lock. I was as clean-cut as they come, athletic, securely employed as a high school teacher and, with the exception of a slight addiction to ice cream, fairly well adjusted. The old man would be thrilled to have me take her off his hands.

Imagine my stupefaction when he wasn't exactly jumping through the phone line to shake on the deal. He didn't really say no, but he sure wasn't handing out cigars or anything. He thought she was maybe a little young and he thought we hadn't known one another very long. He was right on both counts, of course, but I was still cheesed. I felt rebuffed. I don't know if you've ever felt rebuffed, but it's not a pleasant sensation.

Undaunted, I was determined to win him over. I would be charming as hell. He would be unable to resist me and finally would admit, over cigars and brandy, that he had made a terrible error in judgment that no amount of dowry could rectify.

But I botched this as well. I remember, painfully clearly, one of my first Sunday dinners with the in-laws-to-be. Desperate to get in good with Suzanne's father, I was trying to pigeonhole him, get a quick handle on who and what he was so I could apply the soft-soap to the right area.

I knew he lived on a cattle farm, so I said things like "So, how are the cows?" I even tried to feign interest in his line of work, "I've always been fascinated by the canning process. I guess you could say I'm a real can guy."

By the end of the dinner, I was a sweating lunatic and Donald was clearer than ever in his critical appraisal of me. Frankly, looking back on it, I don't blame him. I was an idiot.

Eighteen years and scores of dinners later, I realize where I made my mistake. My father-in-law could not be pigeonholed. He was one of the most complex, multi-faceted and unfathomable men I have ever met. He thought about the state of the world constantly and acutely felt its wounds. As a younger, stupider man, I mistook this depth of thought and preoccupation for addle-mindedness. I thought he was a little dotty. But far from addled, his mind was ever turning and turning, pondering ideas, precepts and philosophies that I, in my self-absorption, had never even contemplated.

Luckily, with time, I matured. And luckily, he waited for me. I loved Donald very much and I miss him immensely. I miss his gentle, thoughtful words, I miss his remarkable ability to listen and to make me feel that what I had to say had merit. And I love him, perhaps most of all, for having the patience to see the germ of a decent man in the idiot who came to dinner.

Dog's Life Away From Owner Not So Bad

My family and I were on vacation last week, snowboarding in the Rockies—the one resort in the western hemisphere, apparently, where it wasn't pouring rain. I came back with sore knees and a big smile on my face. The only downside to the vacation was that we couldn't take the dog along. That may seem like a silly thing to say, but those of you out there who really love your pets will know what I'm talking about.

My dog is a high-strung, high-maintenance, gender-confused lunatic with more emotional baggage than Mariah Carey. He's a canine Richard Simmons. In short, he can be a real pain in the patootie. Having said that, he also never left my side during the eight months of my battle with and recovery from cancer. Outside of the odd Japanese soldier still crouching in the jungles of the Solomon Islands, you just don't find that kind of loyalty anymore. So, naturally, I'm a little anxious when I have to leave him behind for a week.

In the past (with other, more emotionally stable dogs) we have tried the kennel thing. And although I'm not a huge fan of boarding kennels, it worked out OK. But I know that if I left my little canine in a kennel full of barking, nervous dogs, he'd be bald inside of two days.

Luckily, I met the owner and operator of a kennel located on a hundred or so rolling acres of doggie dream world. There are no pens or cages there. There are crates available for dogs that choose to use them, but largely the animals are free to interact and play with one another under the 24-hour-a-day supervision of dog-loving staff and volunteers. At night, most of the dogs curl up in a big, warm pack, snuggled into the heaps of fresh shavings on the floor of the heated and insulated barn. It's a remarkably sensible way to board a dog.

But this kennel won't take just any dog. To get your pooch a spot, you've got to make an appointment and you and your best friend have to pass muster. Obviously, in an open, unchained environment you can't afford to have aggressive, idiotic dogs raised by aggressive, idiotic owners.

Needless to say, when I brought my pooch to camp for the first time, I felt like I was being given the fish-eye more than my dog. I was terrified I was going to be asked some trick question that would reveal my latent homicidal tendencies.

I was sweating bullets. Meanwhile, my mutt was having the time of his life meeting and frisking about with his prospective cabin mates. I started to relax and have fun, too. If you love dogs there is nothing more enjoyable than standing in the middle of a wiggling sea of 15 or 20 of them and marvelling at all of their wonderfully different personalities.

At one point, in the midst of all of this canine play, it occurred to me that, even though the place seemed to have everything a dog and his guilt-ridden, vacationing master could want, there was still something missing—noise. There was no barking. The owner must have known what I was thinking. He turned to me, smiling, and said, "Dogs don't bark when they're happy."

I couldn't have found a better endorsement.

BE POSITIVE AND MEANINGFUL TEACHERS

A million years ago, I was a high school teacher. I liked it a lot and I think I was good at it.

I wasn't particularly brilliant, in fact I once subbed for a Grade 13 math teacher and it was painfully obvious to many of the brighter kids that even on my best day I couldn't find a parabola with both hands.

But what I did have, in abundance, was energy.

I had loads of positive energy which I was more than happy to smear on any kids who'd let me near them.

I still maintain that this is the one thing any good teacher requires.

It's the one thing I ask of my children's teachers.

Pump enough energy and positive light into any kid and they'll do wonders.

It's also why I was completely floored when an acquaintance showed me a piece of art his 10-year-old son had worked remarkably hard on.

Scribbled on the back was the mark "6 out of 10" and the words "could be neater."

That's it. "Could be neater."

Never mind the fact that I think grading any kind of art is a completely ridiculous notion.

Teach them technique; show them oodles of great, soul-stirring art.

But numbers—6 out of 10? Or, for that matter, 10 out of 10!

How does that help this boy love art and discover the art within him?

This guy could've said so many things that might've caught this child's interest, fired him up about creativity and his own abilities.

He could even have been critical, but done so in a way that ignited the child, not dampened him.

"Your use of colour is fabulous. I love it. Next time, see what effect really separating the colours has!" instead of "could be neater."

As it stands, nothing on the back would've been better than those three lazy words. He didn't even have the energy to use upper case.

Imagine walking through the Louvre with a guy like this?

"Oh, Van Gogh. Nice. Mr. Jiggly lines. What, was the guy drunk?"

"Dali, what is that? Like a clock could bend like that. Right. Sorry, 6 out of 10, Salvador."

"I'm not even gonna look at that cubist junk—gives me a headache."

As a teacher, I had my kids write in journals for five or 10 minutes at the beginning of every class. Once a month, I would gather all the journals up, take them home, read them and write back to the kids.

My classes were often noisy but on the day when those journals were handed back you could hear a pin drop. The only sound was the busy shuffling of pages as the kids eagerly skirted to the backs of their books to read what I had written to them.

It wasn't much—just a line, or two or three—but always something positive and personal and wonderful about them. They sucked it up like it was manna from heaven. And it was so easy to do.

Our children may never be Picassos or Monets or Einsteins, but who are we to say? And how will either of us ever know if we don't believe in at least the possibility.

We Could use the Angel of the Overpass Again

Years ago, there was a woman who used to stand on the Wynford Drive overpass of the DVP. In a flowing white robe and a fabulous mane of untamed grey hair that played out behind her in the breezes stirred up by the traffic below, she looked like a combination of Meryl Streep and Charlton Heston. She appeared there, morning and afternoon, during rush hour, facing traffic and holding up the fingers of one hand in a peace sign. That's it. That's all she did. Flashing the peace sign to anyone who cared to look up from their dashboard.

Now looking back from this time, when we are relentlessly bombarded with glaring, glitzy and completely meaningless information from every conceivable medium, the clarity and simplicity of her one-handed message seems starkly refreshing. I miss that old woman.

This morning I awoke to the news of a man who stood on a bridge not far from Wynford Drive, only with a much different agenda than that of the old woman in the white robe. This man was not flashing anybody the peace sign. I don't expect this man had experienced anything remotely like peace for a very long time. He stood on an overpass and threw his five-year-old daughter into the traffic below, then he threw himself to his death, all the while terrorizing the child's mother with a cellphone play-by-play. How perfectly horrible.

Remarkably, miraculously, the child is still with us. Fighting, hanging on, but still, bless her to pieces, with us. What are the odds of anyone surviving a three-storey fall into the express lanes of the nation's busiest highway? And so, I was wondering; I was wondering if maybe that grey-haired angel in the white robe was still around somehow. I was wondering if maybe she had been with that child, protected her with her one free hand, the other still invisibly engaged in its peace mission.

Sound crazy? Any crazier than a world where fathers throw their daughters into traffic? Where men, women and children strap explosives onto their bodies and blow themselves and others to pieces? Where money and oil and power are valued more than fresh air, clean water and happy, healthy children?

Can you blame me for wondering? Can anyone in this world be blamed for yearning for a little outside help these days? We seem to be losing our compass point and I confess that, more and more, I find myself wishing, hoping, that someone or something somewhere still holds the original map of where we're all supposed to be and where we're supposed to end up. And more and more, I find myself wondering if maybe that map isn't already here, in our own hearts, if the directions aren't already plastered everywhere around us; in the coo of a happy child, the warmth of a handshake, the music of laughter. When did we stop seeing them?

I remember I used to drive by the woman on the bridge almost every day and never give her a second thought, unless it was to shake my head and smugly chuckle. I imagine there were a great many of us who did the same thing. But perhaps, given the news we are waking up to more and more these days, we should be paying her a little more attention.

Of Ice and Men—and Kids

It's Easter, a time when we celebrate resurrection, renewal—a return to life after the dormancy of winter.

But I find I am fixated on death—the death of my shinny rink, to be specific.

Before you label me a heretic or blasphemer, know that I am not speaking lightly of this; I have seen miracles occur on this ice. Real miracles.

I have seen neighbours and friends come together selflessly and with joy to put together something they believe will make their town a nicer place.

I have seen sullen, misanthropic teenagers transformed into funny, interesting, kind people on this ice.

I have seen worry-laden, grim adults resurrected as laughing, playful, rosy-cheeked idiots.

I have seen confidence, courage and self-esteem bloom on this ice. Likewise have I seen the mighty and the proud laid low on its surface, courtesy of a well-placed trip or hip check.

And I have personally learned so much from this rink.

I have learned that 150 feet of hose is not enough for a 200-foot rink.

I have learned that you need to turn the water off before you unscrew the nozzle.

I have learned that he who floods against the wind is soon turned into a icicle.

I have learned that the number of children around to help shovel is inversely proportional to the amount of snow that must be cleared.

I have learned that when my wife says she's going to flood my rink for me, I can get just as excited as if it actually were a sexual metaphor.

I have learned that sunrise and sunset are not only the best times to flood a rink but that the winter sky at those times of day will take your breath away and fill your soul to overflowing.

And I have learned that the snotty-nosed kid who is following you around the ice talking your ear off while you are trying to flood will, if you listen long enough and carefully enough, tell you wonderful, important secrets about life and why we are all here.

He will remind you of the child you once were and he will bless you with perspective, and quite probably a cold.

All of this and more from a 40-by-80-foot sheet of ice. Pretty good bang for your buck. Is it any wonder then, that I am having a hard time watching it die?

I know that it will, God and climate willing, enjoy it's own chilly resurrection come next winter, but that seems a long way off right now.

And I wonder what I am going to do in the meantime. Where I am going to go for my inspiration?

How am I to get my sunset and sunrise hits of spiritual revelation, my lessons on childlike perspective?

And most important of all, I wonder what the hell am I going to do with 150 feet of hose?

I Was Under the Knife One Year Ago

It's difficult to believe, but exactly one year ago today, I was lying on an operating table with a pair of strange hands poking around inside me. An hour or so later, I gave birth to a bouncing, baby tumor. It's a momentous anniversary to be sure, worthy of celebration. I'm just not sure how one goes about that.

What exactly is the one-year tumor anniversary? Paper? Saline? Plasma?

And more importantly, what exactly should I do to celebrate it? As the Wicked Witch of the East was so fond of saying "These things need to be handled delicately."

My first thought is that it should be a very personal time between my surgeon and me. I mean I don't know how much more intimate you can get with a person than actually having your hands inside them. Do you think handling somebody's colon counts as getting to first base? Again, I'm unsure. This is new territory.

Anyway, I picture the two of us having a romantic dinner in the hospital cafeteria, the place where we first met, staring happily into one another's eyes as I order for the two of us. "I'll have the stewed prunes and the doctor will have the gelatin…and a bottle of your best flat ginger ale as well."

I wonder how my wife will take it when I tell her "Sorry honey, those flowers are for Dr. Stewart."

Seriously though, it does feel like something should be done. I'm alive thanks to that surgery. We go to a lot of trouble and expense to celebrate other events not nearly so worthy. Grey Cup parties, Halloween parties, Pancake Tuesday. Pretty diluted fare.

How come we don't hear about kidney transplant parties, Bypass Day or Shunt Wednesday?

And can you imagine how busy men's calendars would be if we celebrated Circumcision Day? Or would that be a day of mourning? I don't know. Like I say, these things are tricky.

What I do know is that my life was not only saved one year ago, but irrevocably changed. That surgery set in motion a chain of events that is still active and still transforming the way I look at the world, in a very positive way. Who could've known that I'd come out of abdominal surgery with better eyesight?

My friend Ray, who has been through his own battle with cancer and was always there for me throughout my adventure, once told me that he and his wife made a point of celebrating everything along the cancer journey. They celebrated getting out of the hospital, the first finished week of chemo, the second finished week of chemo, the end of chemo, the last needle and so on. I think that's a good way to go through life.

I think we could all stand to celebrate a lot more and a lot better. We need to stop and recognize milestones, however small. Make speeches, blow out candles, raise glasses. We need to keep reminding ourselves that we're winning, we're still here. And if that isn't worth celebrating, I don't know what is.

There's Nothin' Like a Good Hardware Guy

Right after an understanding wife, every man should have a good hardware guy. And by hardware guy, I don't just mean some clown with his name on a polo shirt and a pencil behind his ear.

There is so much more to being a real hardware guy than just knowing your way around a tape measure. To be a real hardware guy, you have to know how to deal with people like me, for instance. People who walk into your store holding up a piece of plumbing and say "Should this have come off?"

People who pronounce the *l* in solder. People who giggle when they talk about male and female connectors.

I have a real hardware guy, well two actually; they're a father and son team. They even have real hardware guy names—John and George.

You can trust guys named John and George. A guy named John or George tells you you're better off using spiral Ardox than carriage bolts, you're going to believe him. Hardware guys always have monosyllabic names—names like Biff, Reg, Stu or Hank.

Hardware guys also have big hands—hands that have been caught in stuff. If you shake your hardware guy's hand and yours doesn't either hurt, disappear or both, then maybe you should look around.

John and George know me. They know that I don't know a clevis pin from a ball peen.

I've made that patently obvious to them on many occasions. But they also know that I am a man and, as such, am acutely allergic to looking like an ass. I am also stubborn and slow to admit when I don't know something or am just plain wrong. I generally have to bleed or burn myself before I seek outside help.

They know all this and, because they are true hardware guys, they know how to handle me. They never talk down to me and they never laugh—at least not in front of me. Most importantly, they are not hardware bullies.

When I have studied for hours and finally mustered up the courage to ask them for a quarter-inch Fetzer valve, they never say crippling things like "flanged or un-flanged?"

They have mastered the art of what I call steering the idiot.

They are able to take my childlike scribbles and poorly articulated ideas and make them into doable, simple realities. More than that, they make me feel like much less of a dope than I was when I walked in there. They are patient, good-humoured people who smile and indulge my actor's bravado when I am feeling my hardware oats and am bandying about terms like co-ax, chop saw and flux in completely inappropriate ways.

When a man is at the end of his rope, when he has come to a point where he must admit he can go no further without help, he is in a very delicate, uncomfortable place. Wrapped up in that bookcase, or deck or bathroom vanity are great gobs of his self-esteem and pride. Hardware guys know this. Hardware guys live in that place. Bless them.

Only Love Can Get You Through the Pain

As I write this, dear friends of mine are preparing to bury one of their children. And though I weep with them and for them, the depth of their grief is, frankly, beyond my imagining.

Bumping awkwardly up against their terrible sadness I have, these past few days in an anemic effort to understand, tried to mentally go there with my own children. But I always stop. It is too deep, too dark, too cold a place to even play visit. The loss of a child—this is not supposed to happen. Our babies are to cry over our graves, not the other way around.

The suddenness of this event crashing into our lives in the midst of a blessedly beautiful spring Saturday has reminded me of what a tightrope we are all walking. We make our way through this life not looking down. But occasionally tragedy noisily enters and we stumble and freeze upon the rope and for a few heart-stopping moments our eyes shift downward. There is no net and what we thought and felt was thick braided hawser beneath our feet is, in fact, razor-thin monofilament stretched to breaking.

What is it then that keeps us from falling—from plummeting into the darkness of despair and hopelessness? It must be love.

Even as I held my friend in my arms, his body vibrating with a sorrow so profound that there are no words for it, his eyes hollow with disbelief, still there was love. Even as their hearts are broken again and again and again at the merest thought of their beautiful lost boy, there will be love. There is always love. It is at our core. It is all we are.

I ask myself how will my dear friends keep walking on the tight-rope? How will they find the strength and will to take those first few steps, to keep on moving through this time and on into the joy and glory and sorrow that the rest of their lives hold for them? Indeed, how will any of us continue on in the face of this unspeakable darkness without fumbling and falling? Love.

We keep the balance in our lives with love. We fill our hands and our hearts with it in equal measure. We wrench our eyes away from the darkness and the past and we look with hope to where we're going, to wherever the rope is leading us. And we live with purpose. That rope beneath us is there for a reason. It is a direction we must follow. To step randomly and without reason is to fall. To stand still for too long is to fall.

Daniel's death and the black hole it has left behind in so many lives is something for which I have no answer. My soul may understand it but it is not telling. It is strangely quiet these days. My heart, though, is speaking loudly and clearly. It is telling me what it always tells me—love. Get out there and love. Keep moving and love. Love and don't dare stop until the sun comes out again.

All That Sweet Music Just Pickup Lines

One of the things I love about the spring is the bird song. Even before first light, the neighbourhood is full to bursting with the most beautiful music imaginable. At no other time of the year is it so full and lush as it is in these first few weeks of spring.

In the winter and fall, all we get are the occasional irritable bark of a jay or quarrelsome squeak of a chickadee—the avian equivalent of "Dammit, it's cold!" or "Stay here for the winter you said, with everybody else gone south there'd be more food, you said!" Even in the middle of the summer, the heat and humidity seem to take some of the zip out of our feathered friends.

But now, in these days when fresh green life is bursting out of every blade of grass and tree bud, it's a veritable orchestra out there. A friend of mine pointed out that the main reason for the ruckus is that the birds are mating. The noisy chatter and music we hear is, in essence, a kind of treetop bar-hopping. Whoever is loudest gets the hottest chicks, so to speak. It'd be fun, wouldn't it, if we could translate what was being said in all that warbling? What kind of pickup lines do you suppose they use in that world?

"Hey, c'mon baby, it ain't the size of your beak, it's how you use it."

"That's only my country nest. I got a beautiful place in the city."

"Whaddya say you and me blow this dump and go get some worms?"

"Nah, migrating's no big deal when you've done it as many times as I have."

"Say, are you molting or are you just glad to see me?"

"What? This scar? Just some nosey cat I had to put in his place."

"Tufted Titmouse huh? Interesting handle."

Whatever they're saying, they're saying it loud and often from dawn to dusk. Thankfully, it sounds lovely.

But could you imagine what it would be like if we humans courted with the same volume and intensity for these few weeks of the year?

Every day in April you'd wake up to hoarse male shouts of "Look at my lawn mower, look at my lawn mower!"

"I gotta big bass boat! I gotta big bass boat!"

"I'm loaded! I'm loaded!"

Men would put on their best outfits and stroll and strut about town all day long, desperately hoping to catch the eye of available females. Frenzied males would race up to single women, proffering arms full of everything from choice cuts of meat to impressive spreadsheets to homemade patio furniture, shouting "Lookee what I can do!"

As for the women, they'd flit from restaurant to restaurant, eating pricey meals, looking bored and wading through their suitors hoping to find someone who looked like they had good genes, who wouldn't mess up the nest too badly and who wouldn't split too early after the kids came along. Good thing we're not like those dopey birds, eh?

It's taken me almost 45 years, but I just got back from my first hockey tournament weekend. I am different now.

I don't, however, recommend waiting 45 years for your first hockey tournament weekend.

It's a rite of passage that can be painful, both physically and mentally.

For starters, it's going to take a few days—maybe weeks—before I re-acclimate to civilian life. I suddenly have to try very hard to keep the F-word out of my daily conversation.

For three glorious days it flowed out of me like poetry. At the beginning of sentences, at the end of sentences, in the middle of nouns, verbs and ad-F-ing-jectives. Sometimes it just sat there all by it's wonderful self. Sometimes all I needed was the F-word. Now I have to edit myself. Asking the kids to pass the F-ing cereal may be fun but my wife frowns on it.

Secondly, I ingested so much fast food, sugar and trans fats over those three days that I may need to enlist the services of a priest to rid myself of the demons now living inside my digestive tract. The only thing I consumed that was even remotely green were some dill pickle flavour chips. There are things in my colon now that I will more than likely not see again until my mid 50s—chemicals and additives not normally found outside military labs.

And I drank beer. A great deal of beer. Not to excess mind you, but excess is a relative term. I don't generally drink a great deal of alcohol, but remember, I was with a group of men. Groups of men sometimes do silly things.

The Spanish Inquisition was a group of men; the Titanic was sailed by a group of men. And, of course, what is the NHL, but a group of men?

Anyway, while I was never drunk, my kidneys were working harder than a Third World sweatshop. I belched constantly, pausing only long enough to get the F-word out. Still, I managed to maintain a wary vigilance at all times. It is never a good idea to drink oneself to vulnerability in a group of men. One is liable to find oneself shaved and on the Internet.

And of course, I stunk. One cannot wear wet goalie equipment for an entire weekend without developing a certain pungency. By Sunday, both I and my hotel room smelled like an abattoir. The cleaning ladies were rushing out of all of our rooms and sticking their heads into dumpsters to get a breath of fresh air.

But would I have missed it? Not on your life.

Yes, I punished my body from within and without, but I will recover. And for all the physical abuse, the weekend buoyed my soul immensely.

I laughed until I cried too many times to count. More importantly, I felt a part of something very special. To the outsider it was only a collection of paunchy weekend warriors. But to those of us in the room, those of us who pulled the same coloured jersey over our heads, who won together and who lost together, who went down bruised and fighting together, it was something bordering on sacred. Thanks, boys.

Hey, Grim Reaper, Take That!

I had one of those moments yesterday. You know, the ones where you very clearly feel the hand of God giving you a whack on the backside. I was on a movie set, shooting a film with Adrian Brody, Bob Hoskins and Ben Affleck—big time Hollywood stuff.

We'd been filming for about nine or 10 hours. The novelty of working with A-list stars was wearing off for everyone. It was getting very hot; the tension was getting cranked up as the day's shooting schedule appeared more and more in jeopardy. Tempers flared.

The craft table was down to wilted veggies and some unappetizing cheese stuff, and there just didn't seem to be as many comfortable chairs around as we needed. Pretty dire stuff. My back was aching because I'd been standing a lot—on account of the lack of comfy chairs. My feet were sore in my costume rental shoes, and pretty soon, as is always the case when you get two or three actors gathered together, we started griping.

I was in the middle of my fourth or fifth reiteration of how sore my feet were when I looked up and saw it. I can't explain how I hadn't seen it earlier. It clearly had been there all day long, as we were shooting right beside Lakeridge Health Oshawa. As I stood there in mid-kvetch, I found myself staring, open-mouthed, into the windows of the oncology ward. A year ago exactly, I was looking through those same windows—from the *other* side.

It hit me like a hammer to the side of the head. The windows are tinted, but I could still make out the chairs, those big, vinyl reclining chairs lined up around the periphery of the room, each one holding a tired, frightened soul.

The world stood very still for me then.

I could no longer hear the whining going on around me or the clinking, clanking buzz of the film set. The only sound I heard was my own heart beating heavily in my throat. I watched the shadows of nurses moving busily from chair to chair, dispensing hope, while the Grim Reaper leaned patiently against the outside wall, bony arms crossed, a cigarette dangling from his grey lips. He looked over at me and winked.

Suddenly, I wanted to cross the street. I wanted to push him out of the way, rush into the cancer ward in my makeup and costuming and shout "Look! Look! It's me! I was here. I was one of you! But I'm OK now. I'm better! You will be too! I swear you will."

And in that instant, just when I thought my heart would burst through my chest, I was swept back to the present. And, like Saul on the road to Damascus, I opened my eyes and saw the world around me once more with perfect clarity. I felt like Scrooge waking up and finding out he has not missed Christmas morning.

I shut my mouth, smiled hugely at my complaining companions and walked—no, *skipped*—over to the craft table for some delicious veggies and cheese. Then I sat down on the grass, the beautifully cool, green grass. I closed my eyes and, tilting my idiotic face heavenward, said a quiet "Thank you."

Dad Is a Tower of Strength and Love

Sometimes I can't help but think that I was adopted. I love my dad enormously and we're very good friends, but I wonder if we share any of the same DNA.

My father is closing in on 80 but he is still a bull of a man. He's barrel-chested, has hands like vices and forearms that Popeye would envy. He has wrists thicker than my ankles—even his head is big. He has enormous presence.

Not once, even at the height of adolescent insanity, has it ever remotely crossed my mind that I might be able to take the old man. I was a strong kid but he would've folded me up like a beer can. He still could. My dad wears power like aftershave. I wear some fruity smelling concoction with two *u*'s and an umlaut.

While we are both voracious readers, my dad's books all have titles like *Guts on the Beach, Holster Full of Death* and *Armageddon in Heels.* My night table is covered with such page-turners as *Scratch Your Inner Itch, Weed the Hate From Your Garden of Love* and *It's OK to Run Away.*

When my dad had a hard day, he would come home, have a slug of Scotch, then disappear down into his shop where he could saw things, cuss and look at naked women in calendars.

When I come home after a hard day of acting (and yes, I know what an oxymoron is) I have a glass of milk and cookies, then do some yoga—and think of naked women in calendars. If I'm really ticked about something, I meditate.

My dad never meditated—he simmered to a rolling boil. As kids, if we ever saw the old man sitting in a chair with his eyes closed and breathing deeply we got the hell out of the house; that meant he was going to blow soon. On the weekends my dad was never happier than when he had a pry bar, shovel or a wheelbarrow in his hands. He could make a patio stone so level you'd be afraid to walk on it. He could put an edge on a flower bed that'd cut your fingers.

My idea of yard work is lying on the grass with the kids and making shapes out of the clouds. I talk to plants and trees. I can get all weepy if I stand in front of a rosebush for too long. It's no wonder that my dad is so fond of my wife. They're cut from the same cloth, those two.

Suzanne will sit in the garden with me for about five minutes before she has to get up and fix something. That's one of the reasons I don't think I should ever buy a house with a shop. She'd be down there all the time, sawing and cussing and staring at naked men in calendars.

When I think about how different we are, I am struck by how much patience my father must've had with me as a child—not to mention trust. Love, after all, is sticking your hands under a patio stone when the kid who's holding it up is making shapes out of the clouds overhead.

Bike Ride a Return to Youth

My youngest son invited me out for a bike ride the other day. And, although I had one or two more important things to do, I decided to drop them and take him up on his offer. I've learned over the years that when a kid invites you to do something you should jump at the chance. Mainly because I really believe that God is talking to us through our kids all the time, shouting life instructions at us, pointing out significant road signs, trying to get us to see what's really important down here.

Play with your kids for a while and you'll very quickly see what I mean. Five minutes of blocks or colouring and you'll find yourself staring down the barrel of an embarrassing life lesson or two; share your stuff, play fair and it's no fun unless everyone takes a turn being "it."

The other reason I always try to be there when my kids ask is that someday, and that day is coming very quickly, they will stop asking. Dad or Mom will no longer be the focal point of their lives. This is all natural and good. And, frankly, I don't think I want to go through the experience of having my 18-year-old ask me if I want to tag along to the peelers. I don't think I'd have a good answer for that one.

So, my son and I went for a bike ride. Right away I found myself on a pretty steep learning curve. Virtually all of my bike riding for the past 20 years, and there has been a lot of it, has been training.

Clipped into my pedals with my riding shoes, I rode my bike hard. I rode to get my heart pounding, to break a sweat. No pain, no gain.

I hardly ever put my feet up on the handlebars or laid rubber or, God forbid, went no hands.

I had to relearn these things. The hardest lesson, though, was that bike riding is not about finishing.

It's a bike *ride*, not a bike *race*. Kids don't ride bikes to get fit or to test themselves or for personal bests. They're all about the journey. Most of the time they don't even know where they're going.

Respond to "Wanna come for a bike ride, Dad?" with "Sure. Where're we going?" and you'll get a look like you just grew a second head. Bike riding with a kid is very Zen. There is no future or past on a kid bike ride. You're just where you are, in the now. You're not worried about where you're going or where you've been.

We felt that warm summer breeze through our hair. And more than anything, more than the singsong chatter of idle bike talk, or the laying rubber or even the no-hands, that wind through my hair was God talking to me.

Twenty-one Rules for a Grade 8 Graduation

Two days from now I will be sitting in the public school gymnasium watching my oldest son graduate from Grade 8. It boggles the mind. When did this kid, who used to sit in the bathtub and chirp like a little bird at me while I washed his hair, suddenly grow up. His mother took him out to buy some new graduation shoes the other day, and he came back with a shiny pair of size 11s!

He is as tall as her now and there is every indication he will outstrip the old man in short order. This is one of those seminal moments when you can actually begin to feel just how fast the earth is spinning, how quickly the days, months and years are passing. I feel joy, immense pride and some regret. And of course, I feel his hand slowly slipping out of mine.

Like all parents who love their children, I have an immense desire to say something to him, to impart some hard-won wisdom that will make his days ahead easier—or at least smoother. The more I think about it though, the things that I think will help the most are hardly profound. In fact, they're pretty familiar. Still, Duncan, here they are. Ponder some of these chestnuts, my son, as you cross yet another wonderful threshold in your life.

1. Look in the corners for your dance partners, that's where the real jewels hide.
2. No matter how hard you work, play harder.
3. Write your thoughts down.
4. Make everyone laugh and no one cry.

5. Remember on your darkest days, there are always cookies at home.

6. Never forget how to do nothing.

7. Be kind to nerds, they're usually very interesting people and they will rule the world one day.

8. Date at least one girl your mom hates.

9. Play a contact sport. The courage and friendships you will develop will last you a lifetime.

10. Make lots of room for music in your life.

11. Don't take any of it too seriously.

12. Unfortunately, you will need some math.

13. When looking for a girlfriend, watch what she reads.

14. Pick your friends for their hearts, not their haircuts.

15. Date at least one girl your dad loves.

16. When it comes to falling in love, go big or go home.

17. Remember how bad a broken heart feels and be gentle with someone else's.

18. The homework is never as important as they tell you.

19. Let the cool kids peak in high school. Go for the long ball.

20. Remember, when it seems like the future holds nothing for you, you can always be a guidance counselor.

21. And finally, I would like to tell you that you have nothing to fear in this life. You are on your own path and you cannot *not* get to where you are headed. Underneath it all, there is nothing but love. Just enjoy the hell out of the journey, my boy.

READING PULP FICTION HELPED AT DARKEST TIMES

Next to physical intimacy, reading has to be my favourite thing. If I could just find a way to combine the two without hurting my wife's feelings, I'd be on top of the world.

I read whenever I can. I never leave the house without a book or two stowed in my satchel or a paperback in my back pocket, and still I never have enough time to read all the books I want to. My bedside table must have a half-dozen books piled on it, all in various stages of ingestion.

I think it's important not only to read a lot, but to read widely. We all know people who will only read literature. These are terribly dreary individuals who refuse to even consider a book unless someone has hanged himself in it somewhere or one or more children have died in a fire or car crash—or perhaps both. To them, a book is not worth reading unless they feel absolutely wretched upon finishing it. These people were either spanked too much or not enough as children.

I'll read anything I can get my mitts on from Dr. Seuss to *Dr. Zhivago*. Sometimes the cheesy stuff is the best of all.

When I was laid out with cancer, I discovered pulp fiction. I would immerse myself in plots so shallow you'd scrape your knees on the first page. Books where every chapter ended with a guy hanging from a cliff or a nubile heroine surrounded by drooling maniacs, or a maniac surrounded by nubile heroines. I didn't care. Those books got me through some pretty rough afternoons. They took me away.

I have friends of mine who used to pass long car trips by reading Louis L'Amour novels out loud to each other. I've tried it.

I dare anyone to read a Louis L'Amour western out loud and not be in stitches by the end of a chapter.

"Buck reached a muscled arm to take the ladle of cool well water offered by Rebecca. As the blazing sun beat hard upon the mesas, her bosom heaved."

You have to love that. As far as I'm concerned, if you can get heaving bosoms and a gunfight into the same paragraph, you're a genius.

Finally, I don't know whether it was due to improper toilet training or some festering anxiety disorder, but, for the longest time, if I started a book I had to finish it. No matter how bad the book, how much I hated it, I felt I had to read it all the way to the end.

I would lie in bed, book in hand, complaining to my wife, "Man this stinks. I can't believe how bad this is."

I would do this over and over again, sighing and shaking my head, completely ruining her reading experience, until finally, bosom heaving, she would take the book and fling it out of my hands.

I'm better now. I have a rule. I give a book 50 pages to hook me. If I'm still struggling at that point, out she goes. Although, occasionally I'll hang onto a bad one—just to get my wife's bosom heaving. A guy's gotta have some fun.

LOS ANGELES—A NEVER-ENDING SEARCH FOR NORMALCY

In a slight variation on the old joke, "I just flew in from L.A. and boy is my soul tired," I've travelled to the city of angels several times and the place never fails to disappoint. It's a town built on values and philosophies as shaky as the tectonic plates beneath it. There doesn't appear to be anything real about Los Angeles. It's like a giant film set; everywhere you walk you half expect some guy to jump out of the bushes with a clapper board and yell "Take Two."

Nevertheless, I was determined this time around to shelve my skepticism and find enjoyment where I could. The task proved more daunting than I could have imagined.

I thought, for instance, that I might find some pleasure swimming in the rooftop pool of the hotel. It was a lovely spot that afforded a view of both West Hollywood and the hills of L.A. It was also, unfortunately, on the same level as the formidable layer of smog that hangs like a brown blanket over the city. The locals didn't seem to mind it at all but for a Canadian boy used to inhaling crystal clear country air it was absolutely noxious. I had a sore throat inside of an hour. I couldn't see myself spending too much time up there, short of lying on a chaise-lounge in a haz-mat suit. Also, the hotel, apparently, was the destination of choice for actors and would-be actors visiting Los Angeles. That meant that the pool was forever ringed by sculpted bodies with more plastic in them than the *Six-million Dollar Man.* I saw one woman with so much silicone in her upper deck that she could do a cannonball and not break the surface of the water. I knew I was in the wrong crowd when I realized I was the only one there reading a book with no pictures in it. So much for the pool.

The next day I spied a notice for a farmers' market in town. "Aha," I thought, "that's where I need to be. Talking to some people of the soil—salt of the earth types."

I walked down to the market and instantly felt better. I stood gazing at row upon row of the most beautiful produce the California sunshine can muster. I approached a friendly looking man in overalls and straw hat—a real farmer if ever I saw one.

"Hi, I come from farm country myself," I offered, "where's your spread?"

"Out in Modesto," he replied.

"Must be beautiful," I said.

"Yup. What brings you to L.A.?"

"Oh, I'm an actor. I'm working on a film."

I realize now you should never say "I'm working on a film" to anyone in Los Angeles. You might as well say "Open Sesame" because as soon as those words leave your lips all kinds of bad things can happen to you.

My erstwhile farmer friend suddenly broke into a huge George Hamilton grin, put a hand on my shoulder and said, "No kidding? You know, I've got a screenplay I've been working on and it's…"

I never heard the rest of it. I was running like a madman towards the east, towards home.

PRETEND BOWS BEFORE THE PROFESSIONALS

The other day I had to have a flat tire repaired. I removed the flat and put the doughnut tire on myself and I'll admit I was feeling pretty darn masculine at that point. I was out in the sun, sweating like a man and cranking a vehicle up on a jack. My fingers were covered in real dirt and grease—not the makeup kind I usually have applied in a trailer. I even managed to curse a few times during the procedure. Pretty manly stuff for a guy who pretends for a living. I was feeling my oats.

Why then, did it take just five seconds of talking with a *real* mechanic for me to start feeling like a sissy? I hate when that happens. And it starts as soon as I pull into the gas station.

Maybe it was my wardrobe. Mechanics wear grease-stained work pants, baseball caps with grimy finger marks on the brim and big steel-toed work boots. They are all business. I got out of the car wearing a tank top, bathing suit and Birkenstock sandals. The only thing missing was a feather boa.

Plus, I think a big part of my problem in these encounters is my natural curiosity. I am endlessly fascinated by things I have little experience with. Carpenters, crane operators, adult film stars—I can watch them for hours. So, when my mechanic friend started the job of repairing my tire, something about as exciting as buttering toast for him I am sure, I became like a seven-year-old kid.

"What's that for?

"Wazzat thing do?

"Whaddya puttin' that in there for?"

Even as I heard these words leave my mouth I knew I must've sounded like a knob to this guy. I certainly looked the part. But I couldn't help myself. I never can. It's only through massive amounts of willpower that I am able to keep myself from blurting, "Can I try? Can I try?"

To make matters worse, the only reply I could seem to come up with whenever he patiently explained what he was doing, was "Cool." Although it usually came out more like "Cooooooool."

And of course, whenever I tried to dig myself out of this behavior, I only compounded the problem. For instance, I would try to raise my status in his eyes by brilliantly stating the obvious.

"Oh, so you just snip 'er off right there, do ya?"

"Oh, so that's where she's leaking? How about that?"

"Wow, she sure was flat, huh? Cooooool."

To his credit, my mechanic friend managed to keep a straight face throughout our encounter, although I am sure there were a couple of moments where he must've bitten his tongue clean through.

In fact, all of the mechanics within earshot of my moronic performance retained their professional demeanors throughout.

"Relax," I thought, as I climbed back into my car, "They probably get guys like me in there all the time."

I finally drove away with both my tire and my ego a little better inflated.

It's remarkable though, how much an air compressor and pneumatic hoist can sound like laughter.

Highway Signs Merely State the Obvious

Over the past four or five years, anyone travelling on the Don Valley Parkway will have noticed the installation of a number of large, electronic billboards.

These huge signs, located strategically along the busiest stretches of the route, broadcast information to commuters regarding the flow of traffic. They do this through a complex and very expensive system of cameras and computers that constantly monitor the roadway and provide almost instantaneous feedback of a priceless nature to harried drivers. For instance, you may find yourself imprisoned in the stench and heat of four o'clock rush hour, out of your mind with frustration, when suddenly you look up and a pixilated revelation like "DVP moving slowly from Eglinton to 401" pulls you back from the brink.

And is it possible to calculate how many lives have been saved by these five flashing words of wisdom "Buckle up. Seat belts save lives?" It really is remarkable. If you watch carefully, and generally this is not difficult as the DVP is moving slowly from Eglinton to 401, you can actually see hundreds of people slapping themselves in the forehead and reaching for their seat belts as they pass beneath these splendid reminders. Your tax dollars at work.

"DVP moving slowly…" Yes. We get it. We know the DVP is moving slowly. Does it ever move un-slowly? Wouldn't it be so much more effective if these signs actually gave us information that was helpful or at least told it like it really is?

"DVP moving slowly from here to Eglinton. Smoke 'em if you got 'em pal, you're here for the duration. And you better call the wife, you're not making that dinner with the Feldersons."

Or maybe, "Left lane ahead blocked by some loser who wasn't paying attention while he yapped on his cellphone. Angry? His home phone number is 555-1212."

A little trivia might make the drive home a heck of a lot more bearable as well. Why not "DVP moving slowly…did you know a cockroach can live for nine days without its head?"

If they got really clever, they could even work in a theme here and there. "Don't tailgate…have you had your prostate checked lately?"

I also think those dozens of cameras could be put to much better use. With all of that spying going on I am sure they're seeing a lot of stuff the rest of us are missing. Important stuff. Don't you think those electronic message boards would have a whole lot more watch-ability if we started seeing things like this popping up on them: "Always leave two car lengths in between…and Frank, your wife is fooling around with the plumber," or "Slow down, arrive alive…Sheila, does that blouse go with those pants? What were you thinking?"

I think these ideas have some merit. Right now it just seems like we're spending oodles of money so we can be told what all of us already know. Slow down, buckle up, be patient. So what else is new?

WE MUST STOP WRECKIN' THE LAND

When I was in Grade 7, my social studies class was engaged in a discussion about urban sprawl. It was a warm, spring day and the room was crammed with bored, fidgety adolescents who, frankly, could've cared less about the topic at hand. I, personally, was preoccupied with how Susie Haggerty was suddenly filling out her sweater pretty nicely. There was one memorable moment however, when, filled with some kind of passion the rest couldn't have understood, Norma Horton stood up from her chair and, voice croaking with emotion, proclaimed, "They're wreckin' the land!"

We laughed at her. We laughed her and her ugly duckling manner and her weirdness back down into her chair where she quietly resumed her usual, head down, please-don't-look-at-me posture.

I'm sorry Norma. Those of us who laughed at you that day were jerks. It's taken me 33 years, but I finally understand what you expressed so simply and beautifully. In so many cases, they are, in fact, wreckin' the land.

I attended a council meeting recently where the plan for a new subdivision to the west of town was under discussion. This plan, calling for the construction of some 345 new homes, will effectively double the size of my little community. I find that a little terrifying.

So, apparently, do many of my neighbours. I sat and listened as, one by one, farmers and townies alike sat down in front of the microphone and, sometimes very emotionally, tried to convince our council members that this was a poor plan. I, myself, did not speak. I wanted to, very much. But in the midst of so many cogent and intelligent arguments involving water availability, sewage, overcrowded schools, population density, etc., all I could think of doing was to stand up, heart in my mouth, and croak, "They're wreckin' the land!" It was probably best for everybody that I stayed in my seat.

Besides, there were others who spoke beautifully for me. One such speaker talked eloquently about how it has taken over 200 years to create the charming village that I and my family call home.

With those 200 years comes a wealth of culture and heritage that any future development must embrace if we are to embrace the development. You cannot simply dump a community of 345 homes at the side of a quaint little hamlet, walk away and expect that everything will be hunky-dory. It will most certainly not be hunky and I expect never even close to dory.

None of us who attended that meeting are opposed to growth. Growth is natural and necessary. People need to live somewhere.

What is at the heart of this issue however, is how they will live—sustainably and in harmony with the land and people around us or sprawling thoughtlessly wherever there is space. I think most people, in their hearts, want to live in a place of beauty—a place that is much more than a garage and a TV set in a sea of garages and TV sets. We have that place here.

But like a rare alpine flower, it has taken a long time to achieve and its existence is a fragile one. Any change to the environment needs to be carefully and diligently planned. Otherwise, as my friend Norma so succinctly said, it's just "wreckin' the land."

Originals Just Make You Feel Good

I came out of an audition last week and, as I stepped out into the blazing heat of Yonge Street, I was greeted with the most refreshing vision. There, walking towards me, was a young woman in a lovely pink sundress.

A young woman in a sundress is not, in and of itself, much of a revelation on Yonge Street, I'll grant you. There are hundreds of them. But, what was truly extraordinary about this girl was that she was wearing an eye patch. And not one of your surgical grade, flesh tone, "please don't look at me I just had surgery" gauzy eye patches. No sir. This was a big, black, leather Bluebeard special, complete with a thick headband to keep it in place. She might as well have had a gold tooth and a brace of pistols in her belt.

And that was the charm of it. I was completely captivated by this bloodthirsty beauty. She flounced along, hair flying in the wind, dress billowing out behind her like a mainsail, completely and utterly oblivious to the fact that she looked like she was about to board a ship. I just smiled as she danced past. I couldn't help myself. Rarely have I seen so much style, poise and confidence in one individual. In a world of cookie-cutter fashions and belly button exposing droids, she was a breath of fresh (albeit salty) air.

I've met only a handful of people in my life who I thought were genuine originals.

There was my buddy Kevin, who was the only kid in high school to wear boxer shorts when everybody else was still clinging to bun-huggers.

My old girlfriend's brother, Paul, while the rest of us were dancing like lemmings to disco in the 70s, was listening to Dean Martin albums because he knew good music when he heard it.

And my dear friend, Daniel, whose fiery, wandering spirit tore him out of a marriage and sent him halfway around the world to take beautiful pictures and soothe his restless soul.

I love these people. I love being near them. It seems to me that they are the best of all of us. Such people are unusually happy in their own skins. As such, they have very little interest or investment in judging others. They need nothing from anyone and consequently are wonderfully attentive listeners who make you feel infinitely worth listening to. And finally, they are like mirrors. When you look into one of these people, you see, reflected in the unblemished crystal of their own pure hearts, exactly who you are—shortcomings and all—but always with just a magical glimpse of who you yet might become.

Such people make you feel good. When my lovely pirate breezed past me last week, looking, for all the world, like she might be on her way to a costume ball, I didn't laugh. Ridicule, sarcasm and derision— those ancient, ugly weapons of self-preservation were the furthest things from my mind. Instead, I stopped and watched. The smile on my face and in my heart grew as she sailed off into a sea of turning heads.

I just spent a remarkable weekend with a friend I hardly know, and yet who I am intimately close to.

We have only really met three times yet we are, in a sense, like brother and sister.

We come from widely divergent backgrounds and upbringings. We live in very different settings but we have one very critical bond. Gill is two years in remission from lymphoma. I am almost one year in remission from colon cancer.

Like war veterans or plane crash survivors we speak the same secret language, a language punctuated with immense joy and relief but also with its share of guilt and fear. Both of us have watched friends and loved ones fight and lose battles with cancer while we, somehow, continued on. Both of us have revelled in glorious days of borrowed time and both of us have felt an icy finger down our spines while nervously awaiting CT scan or scope results. Both of us are trying like hell to live and love like there's no tomorrow while working very hard not to think about the possibility of no tomorrow. It's a weird balancing act.

So being together to talk and hug and laugh and cry was a very good thing. It was also a very good thing for our spouses. Cancer has long fingers and it profoundly touches anyone who comes near it. Caregivers have their own unique needs and burdens, carrying the combined weight of the sick and the healthy in the family and always with a worried eye on a future alone.

It was therefore lovely and comforting to see my Suzanne and Gill's Gord instantly connecting and easily sharing so much. At one magical point during our first evening together, the four of us were sitting out on the screened-in porch of Gill and Gord's cottage. Gill and I were engaged in a passionate discussion about some aspect of our adventures when I stopped for a moment and realized that Suzanne and Gord were in the middle of an equally important and probably very similar dialogue. There was some serious healing going on out on that porch.

And that was largely how the weekend went.

We swam and ate and laughed and played with the children and very often we talked about those things that un-cancered people talk about—the weather, our kids, books, our kids. But always and eventually the conversational compass point drifted back to what had drawn the four of us together in the first place.

I'm not a big support group kind of guy. I'm sure they do marvellous things for a lot of people but I've never really been comfortable in that atmosphere.

But with Gill and Gord and Suzanne it's different. It's four people happily hanging onto one another. It's the shared message that it's okay to be scared, but it feels better to be happy. It's survivors speaking the same language.

Granny Brigade Perfect Company

I have a thing for little old ladies. One of the perks of living in a small town is that there seems to be a preponderance of grannies strolling around. Lovely, lavender scented, be-shawled flowers who always have a smile and a chat ready for the giving.

They're easy to spot. I find the early morning hours best. The blue-haired granny (not to be confused with the sour-pussed fogey) is a species that rises with the sun and is most visible between the hours of 6 a.m. and noon. They are frequently found in gaggles of three or four in tea shops, knitting supply outlets and drug stores. The patient observer, if he is lucky, may even see them in their most natural element, prowling produce aisles, squeezing fruit with practiced, liver-spotted hands.

I find the best time to go granny hunting is my morning walk to the store for a Saturday paper. This past weekend was particularly productive. The day was bright with just a hint of fall nip in the air, perfect for grannies in full sweater plumage. Within minutes of loitering in front of the local market, I'd limited out.

I came home with a smile on my face and that beatific, after-granny glow. Immediately my wife knew what was up.

"You've been talking with old ladies again, haven't you?"

"Whaddya mean? I was just…"

"You smell like lilac water and you've got foundation on your cheek."

Oh. Busted.

My wife would never stop me from seeing *much* older women though. She knows how good it is for me.

She knows that it's good for a 45-year-old man to still have to address some people as "Mrs." She knows that when you're feeling blue or a little overwhelmed, a gloved-hand patting you on the forearm can be just the ticket. She knows that in a world moving at light-speed, crammed with vulgarity and sharp edges, that hanging out with someone who remembers a time when things moved no faster than a horse's trot and when manners and courtesy were taught alongside arithmetic and spelling, can not only be refreshing, but soul-saving. She knows that even the dullest person cannot live to be 80 without picking up something important along the way.

What she may not know, however, and what may be the most compelling reason to stop and chat with these dear ladies, is that when I do so, I feel like a little boy again. My grandparents are all gone now. But I have vivid, vital memories of sitting in their kitchens, eating their cookies and drinking their milk—which, by the way, was always fat-filled whole milk and nobody cared. So, I relish the time with my elders.

One of these days my wife's going to worry when I don't come home from my Saturday morning walk. She'll scour the town only to find me blissfully asleep beneath a homemade afghan on some old dear's couch, a half-eaten plate of ginger snaps beside me. She'll open her mouth to protest but she'll be shushed and given a disapproving look by the granny in the rocker beside me.

"Let's let him sleep a little longer, deary. He's such a good boy."

Yeah, that's how it'll go.

Tattoos Are
Location, Location, Location

I've long toyed with the idea of getting a tattoo—not in any attempt to be cool or hip, mind you. I gave up any pretense of hip or cool years ago when I started wearing socks with my sandals. But I am intrigued by the idea of putting something meaningful on my body—besides another person, that is.

And that really is the thing, isn't it? A tattoo is for life. So whatever you put on there had better have some lasting resonance. Forty or 50 years down the line, I don't want to end up a drooling heap in a wheelchair with "Sex Machine" scrawled in sagging script across my man-boobs, painfully reminded of my youthful idiocy with every sponge bath.

I see this kind of gaffe every day. Especially young women who, believing it sexy at the time, get something etched into the top of their rumps only to find, as the years and the inevitable pounds add up, what was once a cute design is now a mural. I wonder if that phenomenon works in reverse? If a sizeable guy, for instance, got "I love Robin" tattooed on his body and then lost a chunk of weight, would he be saddled with "I love Rob" for the rest of his life?

I've thought, of course, about having my wife's name needled on me somewhere, but, as much as I love her, even that is playing with fire. For a number of reasons, some tragic, couples don't always stay together. I have no intention of leaving Suzanne, but if she ever finds my secret stash of Richard Simmons exercise videos, I could be on thin ice. Children are a much safer bet. No matter what kind of mess you make of your own life, your kids will always be stuck with you.

I have a friend of mine with two daughters, Lillian and Olivia. In what I think is the perfect tattoo job, he had a heart painted on each of his shoulders with "Liv" in one and "Lil" in the other. You can't do much better than that. Every time he looks in the mirror he's reminded of the two most precious things in his life and the guys in the dressing room think he's got a couple of women fighting over him. That's style.

One other consideration makes getting a tattoo very similar to purchasing a home—location, location, location. Where on your body do you have it done? The sky is the limit, I suppose. People have tattooed every possible surface on the human body—even *those* places. I can't even begin to think about that. There's not enough single malt in the world to get me to go there. Plus, isn't half the fun of getting a tattoo showing it off?

No, I think I'm more of a traditionalist. A shoulder or an upper chest. Maybe a forearm. Wherever I put it, I'll still be faced with the hardest question of all—finding a tattoo artist who can do a decent rendition of Richard Simmons.

Nothin' Like a Demolition Derby

It's fall fair time again. If he were so inclined, a kid could stuff his face full of french fries and cotton candy and throw up in a different small town every week for the next two months. What a province!

My little town's fall fair has its own unique claim to fair fame. At 152 years, it's the oldest fall fair in Ontario. Of course, a good deal has changed since then. Back in 1853, the midway, while I'm sure still thrilling, was a little less sophisticated. Kids lined up to ride the bumper horses, the crazy, tilty stool and the churn of fate. Young lovers found romance sitting atop the novel, but ultimately boring, Ferris square. And parents grudgingly handed over nickels to kids eager to buy gooey sticks of cotton (the "candy" part wouldn't be added for another 20 years).

Still, then as now, the fair is always a big hit. My personal fall fair highlight has to be the demolition derby—an evening of carnage for the whole family. In my book, you haven't really received the full fair experience until you come home glazed with radiator fluid and sand. I had never been to a demolition derby until we moved up here. I went to my first one under protest, snootily thinking it a barbaric display of violence and wanton pollution. And guess what? It was *all* that—and more. Inside of a minute I was hooked.

I don't know what it is exactly, something buried deep inside our cerebral cortex, something left over from the days when violence was a part of everyday life. I'm sure somebody could explain it to me, but watching guys crunch cars into one another is remarkably entertaining.

For the two or three hours it takes to mash a couple of dozen vehicles to a steaming pulp, I'm a different person. I shout articulate things like "Whoa! D'ja see that!" and "Ohhhhh, baby!" until I'm hoarse. I stand elbow to elbow with beer-swilling, yellow-fingered, tattooed people named Biff, Stu and Babs. Remarkably, for the duration of the derby, I have no urge to deliberately use words they can't understand and they don't want to beat me up. It's a beautiful thing. And exciting? It's like a modern-day coliseum, only the gladiators are driving '72 Dusters and Pintos. It's like a three-hour hockey fight.

And like I say, I'm not really sure why we love it so much. Perhaps it's a vicarious thing. After all, the guys out there in the banged-up beaters are doing to each other what each of us has wanted to do to someone at some point in our driving careers. Whatever the reason, it's popular. I've been going to the derby every year since my initiation 13 years ago and every year it's standing (and ducking) room only.

This year I am particularly excited about the demolition derby. This year I get to host it. I, Neil Crone, a kid from the suburbs of Toronto, am going to be doing the play-by-play for a real, country fair, demolition derby. Am I totally stoked? Can I wait for that checkered flag to be dropped? Does Babs like unfiltered Camels?

I was on my way up the stairs the other night, my head full of thoughts and plans and concerns when, passing an open window, I heard something that caught my attention. I sat down on the top stair and looked out the window. It was dusk and the cool, night air was full of the chirp of crickets, the occasional sleepy bird, the delicate sweep of bat wings and the small tender voices of children. Two young boys, my son and his best pal, were sprawled on the still-warm sidewalk, drawing with chalk and talking. I don't know why the moment held me so firmly. Perhaps it was just the loveliness of the evening, one of those when you can smell the fall coming, when someone, somewhere, has a wood stove going, when life is suddenly very still and very beautiful.

I suspect, however, it had more to do with the boys and with my particular mindset at the moment.

They were, in their simple, joyful chatter, in perfect juxtaposition to my noisy-minded preoccupation. One of the things I have always loved about children is their Zen. Kids are very good at being in the now. While most of us carry around so much baggage we need leaf springs, the past is almost immediately forgotten history to them and they very seldom give any thought to the future. They live, as we all should, fully in the present.

I've heard it said that we are closest to God, to our source, to pure love in those moments when we lose track of time. When we've been engaged in some activity or thought and all of a sudden, boom, we are back in the world and minutes, even hours, have gone by unnoticed. This is where kids, God bless them, live.

Have you never wondered why kids are late so often? Why they seem to have no concept of dinner time? It's not that they're irresponsible or selfish. They are just so deeply in the now that they are unaware of time passing. We might cut them a little more slack if the next time we angrily asked them "Where the heck have you been?" they replied, "I was with God." Which, to my mind, is precisely where they've been.

As adults we are still able to go to that wonderful place too—if we let ourselves. I've been there on a number of occasions. Writing for hours at my computer, so deep in thought that neither my bladder nor my stomach can get my attention; building a deck, completely and utterly absorbed with the task at hand—even playing hockey. Although, to be honest, my experiences with goaltending have more to do with praying than anything else.

And so I sat there that night, nose pressed to the screen, transfixed, osmotically drinking in as much of that innocence, that blithe simplicity as I could. I think it worked too. For a few blessed moments nothing else in the world mattered and I was once more just a kid with chalk in my hand and all the time in the world. I was with God.

Forget hockey, forget football, forget the fights. If you want edge-of-your-seat entertainment, go to a spelling bee.

At 6:45 p.m. we shuffle into the room above the arena and take a couple of seats at the end of the second row. My son toddles up onto the dais to join 11 other kids who are sitting and fidgeting and wondering why they are in here when there is a perfectly good fall fair going on outside. My son looks happy and at ease. He is chatting idly with a couple of kids from his school. On the walk over here I had been filling his head with the concept that this was just for fun and that he needn't be at all nervous about it.

Now, interestingly, I am the fidgety one. With a critical eye I size up the competition, looking for something—an edge. I figure the big kid with the 5 o'clock shadow and the sleeveless jean jacket will buy it first. Who's kidding whom? This kid's here because he's dating his teacher or he keyed her car. Either way I'm sure the only words he can spell are the four-letter variety. It's tough to tell with the rest of them. They all look pretty normal, pretty bright. They look, I realize with a sinking feeling, like my kid.

Now it begins. One by one the kids step up to the microphone and face the music. Round one is inconsequential, an obvious gimme to let the kids get their sea legs. Even Jean Jacket breezes over *camel*. Despite the second round dispatching two unlucky competitors, I am miffed. I snort in audible disgust as my kid sweats his way through *caterpillar* only to have the egghead beside him get handed a gift-wrapped *suitcase*. My wife shushes me. She obviously doesn't get it. Our son has a shot here.

I am sweating profusely. We're down to three and, in spite of the blatant bias, my boy's still in the thick of it. But it's not going to be easy. Some brainiac from the other school is hotter than a two-dollar shotgun. She's definitely in the zone. She's halfway through *calendar* when it occurs to me I am holding a camera in my lap. I raise it up and am about to set off the flash when my wife's nails dig into my thigh.

It's stiflingly hot. We catch a lucky break when a wailing baby causes kid number three to put two *r*'s in *sergeant*. "Tough luck pal," I murmur through a grin that would make the ugliest of hockey parents look like Albert Schweitzer. Now it's a tennis match. My kid and Brainiac, volleying words back and forth. The tension ratchets up with every syllable. My son falters halfway through *celery* and my heart stops, my blood freezing for the eternity it takes for him to stammer out "e-r-y."

And then, in a blink, it's over. The girl drops one letter from a word I don't even remember and suddenly I am the champion! That is, my son is the champion. As we head out the door, trophy in my hand, I notice the second-place finisher walking by with a storm cloud over her head. "Geeze," I whisper to my wife. "Some people take these things so seriously."

No Bull, It's the Biggest Steer
I've Ever Seen

I was out driving this past weekend and I happened to pass a field full of beef cattle. No big deal since usually, in my part of the world, you can't throw a stone without hitting a Hereford. Just don't get caught.

But this time around something grabbed my eye that made me slow down for a closer look. In the midst of this slowly shifting sea of hugely muscled animals, there strode a Goliath; a giant among giants—a bull. He was magnificent. He was easily a foot higher than any other beast around him and with his massive hump and what I can only describe as truly impressive tackle, he was definitely *the* man.

You have to see one of these things to really understand what I am talking about. They have an unbelievable presence. I parked the van on the shoulder to get a better look. He stopped what he was doing and slowly and deliberately swung his locomotive of a head towards me. I don't speak bull but his message was perfectly clear. He was telling the big shiny metal thing to back off, these were his women.

And I don't mind telling you, even surrounded by steel and protected by a fence, when that guy took a half-step forward and fired a warning snort in my direction, my hand went for the ignition key. These animals do two things and only two things; and they do them very well. He'd given me a taste of his talent for belligerence, now he proceeded to show me why they call him the "Love Machine."

As he lumbered from wide-eyed female to wide-eyed female I felt a little like a person driving by a car wreck. I knew I really shouldn't look, but I couldn't help myself. The act itself is an incredible blend of romance, violence and a kind of athleticism that defies the laws of physics. It's what you might end up with if you combined a railroad hump-yard with a Barry White concert. Although the audio portion sounds more like Orson Welles trying to tie his shoes.

Halfway through this spectacle I caught myself smiling. It was not a lecherous or puerile smile. It was more the kind of smile you find yourself wearing when you get a chance to watch your favourite hockey star up close or when you get your first real glimpse of a mountain or an ocean. I suppose it's awe.

Although, in this case I will admit there may have been a trace of envy in there too. Boil any man down to his essence and I'm afraid we're all just like that bad boy in the field. Deep inside every guy, re-gardless of education, manners or culture, there's a bovine straining at the halter. Yes, it's a short life, and all too soon you wind up on a Styrofoam plate in the grocery store, but while you're here man, you're living out loud.

It's just eat, drink, fight and please the ladies 24/7. Come to think of it, I guess it's like being Russell Crowe.

BOOKS ARE A LINK TO BRINGING UP SON

I was tidying up my youngest son's bookshelf the other day and within minutes of stacking and re-shelving everything from picture books to Tom Clancy novels, it occurred to me that here, in front of me, was an 11-year literary history of my relationship with him.

Books are one of the few items I have a difficult time getting rid of or giving away. They are too much like old friends. They are doubly precious if they happen to be an old friend you shared over and over again with a burbling, pudgy-fingered infant. And so, going back in time through my son's library quickly became a bittersweet, sometimes emotional, journey.

The earliest strata revealed items from the early era—small, cardboard-paged, sensory books with worn scraps of soft, fuzzy carpeting glued inside them. Next came the peek-a-boo books—books with holes in them, dog-eared from hours of abuse by saliva-coated, arrowroot-encrusted fingers. Books full of barnyard animals, all happily coexisting with the farmer, blissfully unaware of the fall slaughter fast approaching.

Then, as time goes by and parental responsibility begins to kick in, we begin to see themes emerging. Wherever Suzanne and I happened to be on our own particular evolution is clearly spelled out in our choice of reading material for the kids. Here is our cultural mosaic period, with such titles as *A Fatwa for Rusty*, *M is for Molotov* and *Nana's Sweatshop*.

I don't, of course, mean to imply that we've been perfect parents. Far from it. Like all new caregivers, we made our share of mistakes along the way. I still cringe when I think of my kids falling asleep to *The Germans Started It*, or Mike Tyson's *Prison ABCs* or the horrible yet strangely compelling *Too Many Rats*. Live and learn I guess.

My favorite bedtime reads were the *Carl the Dog* books. Carl, an enormous Rottweiler, gets into all sorts of trouble while babysitting his precocious infant charge. These books had gorgeous illustrations but no text. I could, therefore, tell these stories in a different way every night. Sometimes Carl was the hero, sometimes he turned on the kid. Either way the story was very entertaining.

I'd like to think, as I sat on the floor, surrounded by all these gentle voices of the past, that someday my children will pick up a few of these and read them to their own babies. Or, will things have changed too much by then? Will we even be reading books anymore? Instead of crawling up into his mom or dad's lap, will the child of the future simply jack himself into his iPillow and nod off to James Earl Jones's rendition of *Jack and the Bean Futures*? For Carl's sake, I hope not.

PET SPIDER BECOMES PART OF FAMILY

We have a new pet in the family. This summer we adopted a spider. She just showed up one summer day, basking in her newly made web strung over a portion of the back deck. Ours has always been a family that loves to turn over rocks and peek inside bird nests, so when, during an outdoor breakfast one day, we discovered her shimmering there like a jewel on a diamond necklace, we were thrilled. We named her Ruby and we spent countless hours staring at her. Spiders are incredibly beautiful creatures. In fact, I am not even really sure she was a she. I just assumed anything that breathtaking had to be female.

Now, of course, three quarters of our household is of the male gender so it wasn't long before someone, it may have been me, suggested we toss a live fly into her web.

Understand that this had nothing to do with an infantile desire to watch one creature kill another. This was purely about feeding our pet. It just happened to be really fun. I don't know how many hapless flies we caught buzzing around our breakfast, lunch and dinners. But feeding Ruby became a routine part of our meals.

And after a few weeks of our offerings, she was starting to test the tensile strength of that web pretty good. She was a big girl. Still, she moved like a ballerina. Imagine Starr Jones in a tutu. I never tired of watching her work her deadly magic. The minute something live hit that web she was on it.

Her eight slender legs nimbly danced across that silken tightrope in a split second. Then she would grab the fly and hold it while she injected her paralyzing venom. It was ruthless, yes, but never in the least cruel.

I could almost imagine her cooing to her meal "Relax, relax, this won't hurt a bit. You're going to go to sleep. Go to sleep now little fly, go to sleep…"

I don't think I realized I'd fallen in love with Ruby until the cold weather hit. I went out on the deck on a morning so cool I could see my breath. I turned to pay my respects to her and was shocked to see only the tattered remains of a normally pristine web. I actually felt a hollowness in my chest as I searched for her.

Finally, I spotted the tip of one hairy leg poking out from the inside of a curled up leaf on the wall. My heart in my mouth, I reached and gently stroked it with my index finger. To my vast relief, it shuddered and retracted. She was still here. But for how much longer?

Well aware that we may have been interfering with the natural course of things, but unable to help ourselves, Suzanne and I gathered her up and placed her and her leaf in the warmth of the sun on the other side of the house.

I'm no zoologist. I'm not really sure what happens to spiders in the fall and winter. I seem to recall from *Charlotte's Web*, that, having safely laid their eggs, they die. And so, a little amazed at the depth of my feeling for this lovely creature, I left her with her own whispered little prayer, "Go to sleep now little spider, go to sleep…"

Saying Goodbye to Old Acquaintance

I closed a long open chapter of a difficult book yesterday. After spending the weekend with my brothers and my dad, playing poker and closing up the cottage, I drove back with an old acquaintance sitting in the back seat—my brother J.J.'s aluminum walker. After a battle with liver cancer, J.J. died in June, 1982, just six days shy of his 24th birthday.

For a few months before his death he had begun to use a walker to help him get around. Always an athletic, supremely independent individual, he hated it. We hated it too. For the 23 years it hung in the rafters of the cottage garage. It was, for me and I am sure many others, the ugly symbol of an ugly time. I couldn't look at it, for even the briefest glimpse, without a tide of sadness washing over me.

I can't imagine what kind of relationship my father, who spent so much time in that garage, had with it. I suspect the only reason it was kept around at all was because he had used it. For all of its dark mojo, it was still a tie to J.J. and, as the years pass and the rest of our lives unfold, those ties become more tenuous and precious. We are loathe to release them, however misshapen.

But this summer my dad seemed ready to let it go. Ironically, it did not seem to want to go. He had tried to lose it in a series of yard sales but, like something out of a work by Poe, it kept hanging around. Like some four-legged poltergeist, it steadfastly remained while the tools and the knick-knacks and the fondue sets went off with strangers. Perhaps it had developed an affinity for us and the melancholy it brought into our lives.

When I pulled up to the cottage on Saturday it was the first thing I saw—sitting out in the drizzle and the cold, sunning itself in misery, happy as a clam. I think that was when I'd had enough. Suddenly I couldn't wait to be shut of the damned thing. I tore its leg extensions off, stuffed it into the car then walked down to the cottage.

It was waiting for me when it was time to go. It sat in the back-seat and glared at me in the rear-view mirror the whole way home. It seemed to laugh at me. It knew all about my own health issues. It knew all about my fears. It couldn't wait to tell me all about how my brother had suffered. It thought I was taking it home.

I did take it home—I took it to a senior's home. I took it to a place where it was no big deal—nothing special, just another piece of equip-ment, no better than a commode—a place where it wasn't going to scare anybody anymore. You should have heard it squeal as I dropped it off amongst a pile of other walkers and canes. That was the first time in 23 years that I was able to look at that thing and laugh.

LIFE IS SO DOWNLOADABLE THESE DAYS

The other day I was working on my computer and I decided I needed to open a certain application. I had no sooner clicked on its icon when I was notified via a smarmy little pop-up that there was a free, upgraded version of this software available for download. Would I like to download it now? Of course I would. Like most of us, my computer has very successfully turned me into a trained pigeon who will eagerly peck at the red dot to get food or, as the case may be, click for a free downloadable upgrade.

What happened next is what always happens. What was supposed to be a two-second opening of an application to get one tiny little bit of business looked after became a 20-minute install of features I will never use but simply have to have. And I wonder where the day goes?

I sat there, staring at the screen and the slowly inching progress bar. I now measure my life by this slowly inching progress bar.

If my wife calls me for dinner or if one of the boys needs me for homework help, my response is invariably "Be there in 3.2 seconds!"

I began to think how convenient it might be if there were free downloadable upgrades for life. Simply connect a cable into the USB port behind your ear and let the computer and the Internet do the rest. I think I might welcome an email telling me that my career worries were over as version *9.07* of *Talent* was now available. And I know from experience that there are multitudes out there still operating on *Manners 1.0.*

With the various upgrades available, I think it would be informative to see what choices people made.

For instance, which do you think would be the bigger seller, *Literacy 6.05* or *Stud Muffin 4.2? Handyman 7.6* or *Party Animal 9.03?* And how would a woman take it if her hubby gave her *Hooters 9.9* for an anniversary gift? Or for that matter if she gave him *Cuddling 3.5?*

Do you see where this is going? Computer software and its staggering rate of obsolescence has created within the human race a feeling of never being satisfied, of always feeling we need something newer, something better. And that if we are only patient and loyal customers, that newer and better version will come along very shortly. And our lives, consequently, will be infinitely better.

I believe we are improving. I believe we are, contrary to what we see on CNN and the front page of the *Toronto Sun*, getting better as a species. I think things can't help but get better. That's the plan.

But I also believe it is vitally important that we not download every version of this or that into our lives simply because it is free. We need to make choices that serve us, that evolve us, that make us and this planet better. Perhaps if we are looking for things to download they should be labelled *Love 9.0, Kindness 8.8* or *Tolerance 7.02*. Interestingly, these upgrades have always been available and they've always been free.

Thankfully very few of us have any real yardstick by which to reference the horrors of the World Wars.

We can read books and look at pictures until we're blue in the face but we cannot ever know what it was really like—a good thing and a bad thing. Good, of course, in that we have been spared the soul-strangling nightmare of the trench and bombardment and mutilation. Bad in that, if we have not already, we will soon forget the lessons written in blood and bone by so many.

Already generations of children have been born who can read and write and drive a car but who have no real connection to or understanding of either of the past century's conflagrations. Names like Ypres and Vimy and Dieppe mean very little or nothing to these children. The aged, blurry photographs of muddied, tin-helmeted little men with strange leggings seem as faraway and unreal to them as cave paintings. These children live in a world that moves at light speed. What are a mere 50 or 60 very tender years ago to us may as well be uncounted millennia to them. War, to these new generations, is something on the television. It is a box set. It is entertainment.

It seems to me that veterans are like tired and frayed ropes binding the rest of us to an ugly reality that we forget or ignore at our own peril. And, as the years pass there are fewer and fewer tear-stained, wizened faces gathered about our cenotaphs. As these old souls leave us one by one, that bond necessarily becomes weaker and weaker. I am afraid of what awaits this world when it has disappeared altogether. When there are no more voices crying "Lest we forget."

In a special place in my home I have photocopies of my grandfather's attestation papers; documents he filled out as a boy of 18, before shipping overseas as part of the Canadian Expeditionary Force in 1916, before wading into the mud and the gore and the gas. In them he agrees to "…be faithful and bear true allegiance to His Majesty King George the Fifth, His heirs and Successors, and that (he) will as in duty bound honestly and faithfully defend His Majesty, His Heirs and Successors, in Person, Crown and Dignity against all enemies…So help me God."

I am haunted by his signature at the end of this oath. It is the chicken scratch of a skinny teenager from rural Ontario. But it is also a blazing torch that has been handed to me from shaking and bloodied hands. A torch that I must not only keep burning, but which I must now seek young, steady, wise hands to pass it on to.

I have, I realize, my own attestation to sign. I too, am duty bound— to my grandfather and the hundreds of thousands like him.

Face to Face Chat the Preferred Method of Communicating

For a person who has always considered himself a fairly forward thinker, I am sometimes surprised by my own conservatism.

One of the things that has been a huge hurdle for me, for instance, has been instant chat programs. If you have a teenager or even a tween in your home you will no doubt know what I'm talking about. These online, semi-private, real-time chat rooms are virtual places where your children can talk with their friends, complete with streaming video if they so choose. It's much safer than your standard open chat room which, at any given hour, has more men masquerading as women than Church and Wellesley—or so I've been told. And the kids love it—*really* love it. Which is why I'm trying to figure out why I hate it so much.

Ironically, one of the things I most chafe against is actually a safety measure; the anonymity. The kids use nicknames or made-up handles when they're online. This is a good idea for obvious reasons. No one in a chat room environment should ever, to my thinking, use their real name or show a real picture of themselves. There are just too many whack jobs out there—or so I've been told.

However, with anonymity come lies, false bravado and often insensitivity. People say things over the Internet they would never dare say over the telephone, much less face to face with a real person with a real name. And for all of its hieroglyphic LOL's and insipid smiley faces, there is very little nuance to Internet chat. All you have to do is recall your first sweaty-palmed phone call to a girl you wanted to ask out to understand what our kids are missing by typing out their passion in a two-fingered staccato. It takes courage to call another human being and possibly face real rejection.

The other issue I have with the nickname thing is that, due in large part again to the anonymity of it all, the names, especially the girl's names it seems, tend to be ridiculously brazen. Standing over my son's shoulder and watching him converse online I do a double take and have to ask him who Sweet Pants is. Sweet Pants, as it turns out, is in Grade 7. That would make her 12 by my count. Call me old fashioned, but I think 12 is a tad too young to have any kind of sweetness in one's trousers.

Then there's Stick Man who I hope is a hockey player—or at the very least, vision impaired.

I have told my kids I would rather have them racking up long distance phone bills, talking one-to-one with a girl, taking an hour and a half to find whatever magic words are needed to work the spell, than sitting in a crowded, phony-filled chat room. To that end, my wife and I don't make it easy for them. We quite obviously stand behind them while they're typing and read the messages. We're intrusive. We make no bones about the fact that when you're talking to people, you're first and always a human being, not an avatar—not a nickname, not even a smiley face.

There are certain things you expect on a flight—bad food, swollen feet, morons cramming steamer trunks into the overhead bins. Other things you never expect—graffiti on the washroom walls.

I was flying somewhere a while back and that's exactly what greeted me when I squeezed myself into that little cubicle to perform the yoga that passes for going to the loo at 20,000 feet. Airline graffiti. How completely perplexing. Where is this coming from? Who pays $500 a seat so they can sneak into the bathroom and scratch obscenities on the wall?

What was even more astonishing was that this message was not, as one might assume, aimed at the airline or carrier in question such as "Air Canada sucks" or "For a good time call KLM."

No, this particular libel clearly stated that Tony H. was willing to engage in unmentionably unsavoury and more than likely physically difficult sexual behaviour.

Unless Tony H. was the pilot or a member of the flight crew, what are the chances of him ever getting this message? I suppose if you're nutty enough or angry enough to want to scribble on the wall of an airline toilet, clear thinking is not one of your long suits.

I was flying steerage on this occasion and so, as I pondered the strangeness of this incident, I wondered if the same kind of thing happened in first class. I concluded that it probably did. Money has never been any guarantor of sanity.

But I suspected that the content of the missives would be somewhat different. Tony H., while still the subject of invective, would probably at least have his social status raised such as "Tony H. can't close a deal" or "Tony H. wouldn't know a good shiraz if his wine club bought one," or "Tony H. drives a domestic."

I surmised, also, that I probably shouldn't have been that shocked to discover this "writing on the wall." Graffiti is, after all, the expression of human frustration. And, therefore, one may expect to find it anywhere one finds his fellow man.

No location or occupation is sacrosanct. From the assembly line "Tony H. solders like a baby," to the Supreme Court "Tony H. has a tiny gavel." People are people and even the most spiritually evolved bump up against things and other humans that upset them "Tony H. has a muddy aura," "Tony H. meditates with his mouth open," "Tony H. is a dirty fast-breaker."

The only real question that remains is why some people feel compelled to share their anger in very public places. I've always been a journal keeper so I fully understand the therapeutic value of writing it out. I just never considered sharing it. The thing about emotions is that they change. Once you write down how you feel about something or someone in public, the damage is done. And what do you when you no longer feel that way? Post an addendum?

"Tony H. is a jerk!"

"OK, I may have misjudged Tony H."

"Tony H. has many redeemable qualities."

"I love Tony H."

SOME PEOPLE JUST CAN'T TAKE A HINT

There is a new website available that purportedly hooks up people looking to carpool. I initially thought this was a pretty good idea. But, the more I thought about it, the ickier it became.

Isn't it kind of like an automobile Lavalife? I mean, I don't always like sharing my car with friends, let alone complete strangers. And let's face it; people aren't always exactly forthcoming over the Internet. What do you do, for instance, when "Fit, young biz exec, seeking lift to King and Bay" turns out to be 400-pound Louie, a 45-year-old guy who manages the fast food joint across from Commerce Court, lives with his mom and can't even spell antiperspirant?

Keep in mind this service is primarily for commuters like me who routinely spend anywhere from one to three hours a day getting to and from work. Remember, one hour of normal time is four hours in annoying jerk time. That's not even factoring in rush hour and traffic jam delays.

When we were living in Thornhill, my wife and I once drove an acquaintance home from a downtown theatre engagement. The guy seemed totally normal. But seemingly normal people often turn into morons the moment you put them in a car. This fellow had a particularly bad case of leaning-forward-from-the-middle-of-the-backseat-and-not-shutting-up-itis.

I guess he was one of those people who simply cannot stand silence in a car. And so he blathered. He had something to say about everything.

"Boy this road is bumpy, huh? Did you know that tarmac comes from the words Tar and MacAdam, the name of the guy who invented it? A lot of people think it's the same as asphalt, but they're mistaken…"

Eventually, realizing we had a problem, we subtly turned up the volume on the radio, but he just matched it with his own. Next, we stopped acknowledging his comments with our head-nods or uh-huhs. He didn't care. He verbally bulldozed his way over any and all conventions of polite conversation. He droned on and on, filling the confines of the car to stifling with his own hot air. Soon we didn't even look at him. That didn't slow him down a whit. Blah, blah, blah, blah, blah.

To this day he is the only human being I have ever seen my wife yell the words "SHUT UP!" at. Around about the 401 she lost it. Had I not been lulled into stupefaction by the constant stream of inanity from the backseat I might have seen it coming and perhaps intervened.

Her fingernails were digging gouges into the steering wheel and her jaw muscles were clenching and unclenching like someone trying desperately not to vomit. Then, suddenly, with the intensity of a cobra striking, she snapped her head around.

Her angry face inches from his jowly, blabbering puss, she let him have it. I can't be sure, but I think, had we not been in the middle of three lanes of 100-km/hr traffic, she would have pulled over and kicked his irritating butt out of the vehicle too. As it was, her message was so frightening that neither he nor I spoke another word for the remainder of the trip.

One of the great things about kids is that they often force us to expand our horizons, to go places we might not have gone otherwise. It's largely in those places where learning occurs, where life unfolds.

Who among us can say they haven't gleaned some life-altering wisdom at the bowling alley, the lizard farm or the video arcade? I recall one particularly instructive outing to a petting zoo that may well have saved my marriage.

But the biggest life lessons come when our children's needs oblige us to visit those unattended places inside us, places we've been successful in avoiding all these years. I recently went to one of those places. There, I came face to face with my inner nerd.

One of my kids has a keen interest in fantasy games. In and of themselves these are healthy, intellectually stimulating and imaginative activities. They involve math skills, multi-tasking and peripheral thinking to achieve success. And once you get used to referring to your child as Hrothgar the Antagonizer or Xuatalpec Bringer of Badness, it's good, clean fun.

The difficulty for me—the really scary part—was going to the store to check the stuff out in the first place. You see, these fantasy gaming stores are like salt licks for nerds. The atmosphere reeks of geek. I wasn't in the place five minutes when I was fighting the urge to do a science project. Everywhere there were guys with glasses and "Pottsie" haircuts; guys wearing slacks that fastened just below the nipples.

I also realized, with a chill, that I was the stranger here—the outsider. I had stumbled into their den and they eyed me warily, nervously adjusting their spectacles and hiking their pants up even further. I could've kicked myself for not bringing along a Nerd/English dictionary. I was suddenly anxious and about to bolt when I heard a voice from behind me.

"You look a little lost. Can I help you?"

I wheeled around. He was obviously an elder—or at least a member of the high council. He wore a red polo shirt and his name tag said "Jeff." When he spoke, the others turned to look, cautiously closing in, mouthing silent algorithms.

"It's not me…" I stammered, "it's for…it's my son. I'm not…"

"Well, let's see if we can't you set up with something."

He smiled and I noticed the glint of…was it an earring? Cool. Jeff spoke with enthusiasm and confidence and, to my great surprise, I found myself liking him immensely. He easily explained the complexities and nuances of fantasy gaming. I became relaxed and, yes, interested.

I began to unconsciously hike up my pants. The others let their guard down and I was able to walk freely in their midst. Jeff led me to a table at the back where an actual game was being played. I soon found myself completely absorbed and even accepted.

There was only one anxious moment where I made an offhand comment to the effect that the Baalim looked a lot like the Zerg. Silence fell over the table. Dice clattered to a stop. Bespectacled heads slowly turned my way. Then, thank goodness, a chuckle. Then another and another and then hands slapping my back and hoots of approval.

These were nerds, yes. But they were also my people and I had come back to lead them.

COINCIDENCE CAN BE A WONDERFUL THING

I've been reading about coincidence lately. Specifically, how coincidences may be much more than simple happenstance or lucky occurrences. That they may, in fact, be signposts pointing us in a certain direction, notices that are flashing around us all the time, in multitudes, if we have the eyes to see them.

I had just such a wonderful coincidence happen to me the other day. I was driving along downtown and I was thinking about Christmas, thinking about how I really wanted this one to be special—memorable. To that end, I was running a bunch of festive scenarios through my head such as taking the family out sledding, or having a huge drop-in with loads of friends and a buffet of culinary delights, or getting everyone on my list the absolute perfect gift.

In fact, I was starting to feel stressed. It was as though Christmas would somehow not be up to snuff if these things didn't happen.

In the middle of this growing worry I stopped my car to let a couple of pedestrians cross in front of me. Two people, a man and a woman, were cruising across the road, side by side, in a couple of those electric tricycles one often sees seniors driving along in.

This was a rough part of town and these two were what one might describe as hard characters.

The woman was gaunt and hollow-eyed with stringy hair, frayed jeans, tattered nylon hockey jacket and unlaced running shoes. The man was overweight and shapeless, unshaven, and wearing a stained pair of sweatpants that showed a generous portion of his ample backside. Both had cigarettes dangling from their lips. I've seen a thousand characters like these two in my daily drives and there was nothing really remarkable about this pair.

There was nothing there that would make me stop and take a second look.

Except, I did notice something.

Each of them had a wire basket on the front of their trike, loaded with goodies. The man had a six-pack of beer and a bag of chips. She had a carton of smokes, a fifth of booze and a bag of candy canes.

They were getting ready for Christmas. Then the universe tapped me on the shoulder. Halfway across the road the path narrowed around a lump of ice. The man stopped and, with an affectionate pat on the woman's back, beckoned her to go first. She flashed him a gap-toothed but loving smile and off they went.

I felt a bit like the Grinch then, straddling Mount Crumpet and suddenly understanding how the Whos could still celebrate Christmas without all the packages, boxes or bags. And just as suddenly my own Christmas slipped gently into its own perspective. What a coincidence.

Do Yourself a Favour and S-L-O-W Down

I was bustling down the main street of town the other day when a young mother and her toddler stepped out of a doorway and onto the sidewalk in front of me. I slowed to accommodate them, and then I found myself just watching and smiling. One of the wonderful things about being a parent to very little children is that you can't do anything fast anymore. They eat slowly, they dress slowly and a 50-yard walk to the post office can, if you let it, take the better part of a morning.

This little guy was probably two or three years old and he was fascinated with everything around him. The snow bank alone was good for two or three hours of investigation and climbing. His mother obviously loved him to pieces and was happy to simply let him doddle and explore while he, chatting like a little bird, excitedly educated her on his findings.

My boys are 11 and 14 and with the exception of tidying their rooms or getting out of the shower, move much more quickly through the world than when they were two or three. But I remember well those days when our pace was set by a pair of size two orthopedic shoes and chubby little fingers that wanted to touch and feel everything around them.

You can't be near that kind of curiosity and wonder and not have a little of it rub off on you. It's one of the most precious gifts our children give to us. I recall, years ago, a trip out west to visit my brother-in-law and his family. We decided that a walk around the sea wall of West Vancouver would be a real treat for the kids.

As we headed out, my guys were immediately enthralled by the seashore and the millions of treasures it offered up. They were forever stopping and running back and forth to their mother and me, arms laden with the rarest of stones, sticks and shells. My brother-in-law, however, was growing impatient. He was used to whisking his own son, born with cerebral palsy, about in his wheelchair at an adult trot. He was a guy who liked to get things done. He'd never learned to stop, look and listen.

One of the nicest moments of that trip was when, once he'd realized the rest of us were going nowhere fast, he dialled it down and joined us. My kids were more than happy to share their findings with their cousin who seemed just as delighted to be part of the noisy tardiness.

At this time of year, things tend to move along at light speed. We push ourselves to multi-task and multi-visit and be multi-merry. But in so doing, we may be missing much of what the season is offering us.

I've always considered the prophet Isaiah a glass half-empty kind of dude. I think somebody really needed to take him bowling or something, but there's no question he hit one out of the park when he said "A little child shall lead them."

Have a slow and merry Christmas everyone.

BIRTH SONG COULD GO SO WRONG

I recently read of a certain African tribe that has an interesting birth ritual. As soon as the mother knows she is pregnant she writes a song for her unborn baby, a song extolling her love for this child, her hopes and dreams for him and what he may become in his life.

This is a very important song and it will be sung to this child by the entire village on the day he is born and then again, many times throughout his existence. The song will be sung at birthdays, coming of age ceremonies, weddings and eventually, one last time, at his funeral. This is a lovely idea and one that we could all borrow and benefit from. I just wonder if maybe one has to be a little flexible with the lyrics now and again.

I mean, as parents, we all have enormous hopes and dreams for our children. We want them to achieve their full potential and to reach for the moon. All well and good. But, in spite of our parental strivings and interference, kids have a way of turning out the way they're meant to, not the way we want them to. And so I wondered if maybe the folks in that African tribe have to fudge the words on occasion.

I'm sure no mother, for instance, on learning she has conceived, sits outside her hut, rubbing her hands over her newly swollen belly, happily singing "Oh, Bruce, you will be short with an overly large head…You will never get a decent job or even come close to killing a lion."

No. She would sing of great deeds and bravery and chiselled good looks.

But, as any parent knows, around the ninth or tenth birthday, the writing is pretty much on the wall. So, what do you sing when, in spite of your every effort, your dragon slayer is a slack-jawed boy?

You fudge the lyrics. "Oh, Kevin, you will do pretty good things… the sun will shine on you and you will learn to use a spoon…you will be a man who buttons his pants well…" You can almost see the chief rolling his eyes, can't you?

Flash forward a few hundred years to our own society and the picture probably wouldn't be that much different. "Oh Steve, you of the mighty paper route…copier of essays and pusher around of kids smaller than you…long will you sit in front of game shows and there is no end to the chips you will consume…repeater of short words and stainer of shirts."

Still, I think it's important to sing to our kids, to remind them continually and hopefully of what they may become and not to berate them angrily with what they have become or probably will become. Or at the very least we may sing to them that, whatever they have it in mind to become, they should do so happily and in the knowledge that they are right where they are supposed to be.

We can't all be dragon slayers, but we can walk our paper routes with a smile on our face.

Uncle's Gift Was One He Never
Knew He Gave

My dad emailed me a week or so ago to let me know that Uncle George had died. I was sad—very sad actually, and it surprised me.

I haven't seen or had any contact with my Uncle George for more than 30 years. Even then I think I only met him once or twice. He disappeared around my 15th or 16th year, leaving behind a wife and kids, friends and a mythic reputation in a young boy's mind.

Kids are like sponges. They eagerly soak up anything their parents say and do. Anyone who has ever had their child embarrass the hell out of them by repeating dinner table talk in the checkout line will attest to the truth of this.

And little boys are particularly hungry for stories from or about their dads. What is a mundane remembrance to us is the stuff of legend to our children. My own boys, for instance, never tire of hearing about my Grade 6 dalliance with evil when Bruce Fader and I flooded the public school toilets. The fishing/hunting trips, the lunatic best buddies, the first cars, the girls and women who rode in those cars— these stories, burnished bright from repeated tellings and retellings, are epic in a kid's mind.

And in this age where sound bytes and headlines are rapidly replacing oral tradition, ritual and storytelling, they are, all too often, the last link to where we come from, who our people are and what we are made of. Important stuff.

My Uncle George was married to my dad's sister. He was my dad's best friend and his best man. They rode motorcycles together when riding motorcycles still made you a bad guy. They took road trips together, they drank together, they got in and out of trouble together. They grew up together.

One of my favorite Uncle George stories took place after a party. My dad and George are driving home. Dad at the wheel and George, a little worse for wear, in the passenger seat. On the seat between them, stowed in an old tin cookie box, was a brand new light switch my dad was intending to install in the vehicle.

In short order, perhaps because of that faulty light, they saw the flashing cherry of a police cruiser behind them. Dad pulled the car over to the shoulder in the middle of a bridge over the Don River. The cop walked menacingly up to the driver's window, leaned in and, with a scowl, asked for identification. George responded by picking up the tin on the seat between them and gleefully chirping "Have a cookie, Officer?" The cop grabbed the cookie tin with its brand new light switch inside and hurled it over the side of the bridge into the swirling black waters of the Don. My dad was furious. George just grinned.

That dumb little story and the man who featured in it have stuck in my mind all these years. It and a host of other, equally dumb, equally little, stories are a big part of the fabric of my life. They are magic. They turn a father into a person with a life and a history beyond me.

Uncle George may have made a mess of his own life in 100 different ways, but I will always be indebted to him for a gift he probably never knew he gave me.

OLD-TIMER PACKING IN
SNOWBALL FIGHTS

One of the few upsides to this ridiculously stupid weather we've been enduring is that there have been a few choice days of sunshine and warmth. Combine those two with some leftover precipitation and you have what is known in the vernacular as "packing snow."

Packing snow—that marvelous substance dreams are made of. All you have to do to get the kids away from the TV set and outside is shout "Hey guys! It's great 'packing!'"

All Canadian kids east of Vancouver know what that means. It's snowmen and snowboard ramps high enough to break your neck off. It's snow forts. It's pitched battles to the death with an unlimited supply of ammo lying right at your feet. It's heaven.

Personally, I've always considered packing snow to be one of the chief reasons I had targets—I mean kids. Some of the best winter memories I have are of me versus a dozen or more neighborhood rugrats, filling the air full of icy, white projectiles, laughing our cans off until someone lost an eye or I was too tired to move anymore. And make no mistake, to a kid a snowball fight against a grown-up is a big deal. When else does the opportunity to hurl things with impunity at an authority figure occur? Never. It's a very special time.

With that sentiment in mind I snuck out the garage door last week to sandbag my youngest and several of his buddies who were already engaged in a conflict of their own. My plan was sound. I would quietly stockpile a half-dozen or so snowballs then storm the enemy, Vimy-style, scattering them; then, in the ensuing panic, neatly pickoff the

stragglers and weaklings. It had certainly worked before. Executed effi-
ciently it might even end in tears. I had overlooked only one small, but
as it turns out, terribly significant detail. The kids had gotten older.

When I roared out from my hiding place, I enjoyed only the
briefest moment of surprise on the kids' faces. After that it was the
charge of the Light Brigade all over again. The children did not, as is
usually their custom, scatter in confusion. No—after the initial shock,
they very quickly hunkered down and returned fire. In a few awful
seconds I found myself out of breath, out of ammunition and completely surrounded.

Then the little buggers opened up. Call me an idiot, but I had no
idea an 11-year-old boy could put that kind of heat on a snowball. I
felt like the 7th Cavalry at Little Big Horn. Finally, one arm shielding
my face, I managed to stagger to a place of moderate safety where I
pathetically tried to invoke some shred of parental control "OK! OK!"
I panted. "Let's have some rules here, all right?" Remarkably, they
stopped.

"All righty," I wheezed, "'Cause there's six of you guys, and only one
of me, I've only gotta hit you once and you're out, but you've gotta hit
me three times before I'm out...'K?"

In the old days this kind of deck-stacking would've raised howls of
protest. Now, they only stood there, silently grinning and tossing their
perfectly rounded balls of death from hand to hand. A freckle-faced
jackal at the back of the pack called out "What about head shots?"

I went in the house.

I've Got the Cellar-dwelling Sump Pump Blues

I have a senior living in my basement and she's driving me crazy.

Seems like every 40 minutes or so I hear her moaning away down there, especially when the weather is wet or humid. She hates the wet. When it's wet or raining she seems to complain constantly and I, as a result, am forever running down there to look in on her, to tend to her.

I confess, in my darker moments I am very tempted to pull the plug and be done with her. But that would be wrong, I know—also very dangerous. You see, I need her. I need her terribly. In fact, if she should ever die, I would be in an awful fix. And my basement would undoubtedly flood. My senior is a sump pump.

I say she is old, but in fact I can't be certain of her age. She was here when I bought the place some 15 years ago. I don't know how old that is in hardware time. If it's anything like dog years she's prehistoric. And with that age comes a pail full of attitude.

She's like some aging diva who won't come out of her trailer, stridently insisting that I come to check on her every hour on the hour or she'll quit the project entirely. And I cannot have that. I've too much money invested in this movie. She knows this.

She also knows, all too well, that my house seems to be built directly over some ancient aquifer. Such is the abundance of water gushing up from beneath my foundation that in the middle of the worst August drought in years—a summer where crops withered in the field and dogs were dropping dead in the street—I could've easily watered 100 head of cattle in my rec room. As I say, she knows all of this. And so we have entered into an ugly, loveless marriage of convenience.

She keeps me dry and I keep her supplied with all the AC she can handle. And brother, can she suck it up. It sickens me to watch the way her eyes roll back in ecstasy when I plug her in. It's pathetic. Once during a brownout, she got the shakes so bad I thought we were going to lose her. I'm not at all proud of this, but I found myself driving around in the rain, looking to score some electricity in some of the worst parts of town. I had horrible visions of getting pulled over and some nosey cop asking me what I was doing with the generator in the back of my car.

I took a huge chance this past summer and installed a battery-powered backup pump. I didn't know how the old fart would take to sharing her sump hole. She gave me the gears pretty good for the first week or so, but it seems to have worked out.

In fact, if my last hydro bill, which could double for the GNP of Uganda, is any indication, it looks like the old lady's got the new one hooked on the juice as well. How sad is that? Not as sad, I'll betcha, as a down-and-out actor who has to knock over a liquor store just to keep his basement dry.

Death of a Horse Shattering

A couple of years ago when my younger brother Tim was training to be a part of the Metro Police Mounted Unit, I had an opportunity to go down to the stables and visit. It was quite wonderful. Wonderful to be around so many magnificent creatures and wonderful to see the change in my brother—to see him falling in love with horses.

I watched him grooming them and talking to them, stroking their velvety muzzles and affectionately patting their massive flanks and necks. I realized then how good this was for Tim—how good it would be for anyone. Animals, especially domesticated creatures, are precious gifts to humans. If we allow ourselves to be touched by them and connect with them, they reward us with life-changing riches.

My brother was then and is still a member of the ETF (The Elite Emergency Task Force.) He is a sergeant and has the safety and care of many people as his responsibility. Daily he faces situations and crises that I can barely write about from the safety of my home. So, it was with great joy that I watched him interacting with these gentle giants, saw the stress falling off him, saw some of the armour dropping away. I know that, even though he has yet to officially join the mounted unit, but has stayed with the ETF where he is currently needed, the bond he created with those horses has never left him. He often drops in to see them, to ride them, to talk to them, to reconnect.

And so it was that I felt my breath being coldly sucked away this past Saturday as I opened the paper to see the photo of several desperate officers draped over the body of a maimed and dying police horse, deliberately struck by a hit and run vehicle. The heartbreaking beauty of that photo has remained with me. It is the essence of love and nobility and sacrifice. Something told me to call Tim then and when he couldn't come to the phone I knew that what was just a terribly sad news story to me was a black hole for him.

The universe moves mountains sometimes to teach us hard lessons. That night, Tim had been on duty and was called to the scene where his beloved Brigadier—his favourite—lay torn and bleeding on a cold, wet road.

He told me later that as he approached the scene he only needed to see that golden tail to know who it was. He told me through a voice taut with emotion about the tears in the eyes of the other mounted officers there, of the gentleness and the tenderness with which they pled with Brigadier to lie still and of the horse's agonizing efforts to raise his once magnificent body to its feet.

And as the precious minutes passed and frantic radio calls were unable to bring a vet and any kind of relief, the universe pointed its unwavering finger and laid its enormous burden upon the weary shoulders of my brother and those other officers there who loved this animal so deeply. The call was made. The shotgun was loaded and my brother, my hero, stroked his friend's muzzle and whispered to him one last time.

So Many Books, So Little Time
for a Club

For some time now I've wanted to start a book club. I haven't talked about it much, especially among my male friends. You've really got to pick your moments for that kind of thing. Nothing stops locker room banter faster than, "Any of you guys interested in coming over tomorrow for coffee and book chat?"

Still, I love reading. I love books and I love talking about books. It's fun and it's good for the brain. The trick, I'm realizing—I mean the real linchpin to these book clubs—is getting just the right people involved.

Book clubs are a lot like fishing trips or poker games; all it takes is one jerk to ruin everything. So you have to be vigilant and very selective going in. Because once somebody is in the club and turns out to be a moron, I don't know if there are any established mechanisms, short of giving them the wrong address, for getting rid of them.

How do you drum somebody out of a book club? Do you just take the honest route and risk hurt feelings? "Sorry Al, none of us realized you were a knob until you wouldn't shut up about Maeve Binchy… you're out."

Or do you lie to avoid a scene and possible bodily harm? "Wow! What are the odds that everyone in the book club but you would go down with bird flu, Al? Oh well, not much point in carrying on now, is there?"

It's a fine line. After all, you want a membership that is fairly diverse. Nothing is more tedious than everyone having the same opinions and tastes all the time. But you've got to be careful. Too much diversity and you've got a donnybrook breaking out over *The Da Vinci Code* or pastry slinging over the *Life of Pi*. And what qualifies as diverse? Do back issues of *Mad Magazine* actually count as a genre?

Finally there is the tricky little issue of gender. Most book clubs that I am aware of are almost exclusively female. That's not necessarily a bad thing. In fact, for months I have been lobbying for membership in a local, all-female erotica book club. I told them we could have all the meetings at my house. I even said I'd supply the crunchy cheese snacks and cream soda. For some reason they've stopped returning my calls.

Ideally I'd like a mix. I think men and women bring varied and interesting viewpoints to the table. There is an innate difference in our world views that makes for provocative, stimulating and, if one can avoid fisticuffs, edifying discussion.

One runs into difficulty, however, with the couples issue. You know, the love him/hate her dilemma? We'd like to have Mary in the group but all Roy reads are snowmobile manuals. George is an intelligent guy, but Phyllis needs a dictionary to get through *Beetle Bailey*. Or even, "Sure, we all hate Tom and Betty, but they have a hot tub and Tom makes wicked date squares." It's all a little daunting.

Maybe I should just join an existing book club. That's if they'd have me. "Oh, sorry Neil, we had a book club, but what with that bird flu and all…"

Green Acres Is the Place to Be!

My wife and I have been looking for a farm now for a while. I love my little village, believe me, but we've been townies for almost 15 years and it's funny how your perspective changes.

I can vividly remember my first night in this old house. I couldn't sleep for the quiet. My body was attuned to shutting itself down to the hum of traffic, the wail of sirens and the glare of halogen light through the window. The sudden silence of a small town was deafening.

Now, after more than a decade here, what passes for silence is a different animal. I am prone to sitting bolt upright in bed and hissing "Geeze! Is that someone walking by our house!" It's ridiculous, I know. I may as well be tossing and turning because the moon is too loud or "those damn ants are at it again!" But it happens to you. In one of life's little ironies, the quieter it gets, the more stuff you hear.

So, yes, I've been thinking that having a little place in the middle of some acreage might be the next logical step. I think my neighbours would agree. I am a bit of a naturist when the weather turns warm and I am sure they have seen more of me than they ever signed on for. When I walk out on my deck on a summer's morning all I want to hear is birdsong and perhaps the babbling of a brook—not the horrified shrieking of women and small children.

A farm may be the answer. Of course, there is one other small issue. The word *farm* can also, unfortunately, be interpreted as a verb. As can the word *ranch*. What I am looking for could probably more honestly be described as a *laze* or a *loaf*.

I have no inclination to farm anything. I am looking for a quiet little place with a shady spot under some huge old trees where I can sit with my notepad and perhaps a tasty mint julep and watch someone else farm. That would be my ideal.

Regrettably, I am not sure my wife and I are on the same page concerning this farming thing. Suzanne was raised on a farm and is, as I have noted before, happiest when digging, chopping or welding something. Even in our most intimate moments, I get the feeling she is thinking not so much about what a great lover I am, but how she needs to plaster those cracks in the ceiling.

And that's OK. In fact it's great. The two of us have, in 20 years together, worked out a pretty equitable system. Over those years I have, I hope, taught her a thing or two about the gentle art of loafing and she has unquestionably shown me on many occasions that there is great satisfaction in hard work well done.

And now that I think about it that may be the best reason yet why a farm is a perfect fit at this point in our life. Those moments of stillness, of sitting and relaxing and listening to the world from your verandah are always made that much sweeter when you've earned them through a little work. Mind you, I did say a *little* work.

You've Got to Rely on Love

Sometimes the job of parenting is as easy as falling off a log. Other times it's more like trying to build a space shuttle out of Lego with no instructions. Sometimes I think I've got it all figured out. I'm Ward Cleaver, Glenn Ford and Bill Cosby all rolled into one.

Other times I'm surprised anyone would trust me to babysit their hamster.

It's hard, this parenting thing—mainly because it's a moving target. Just when you've got a handle on feeding and changing and burping, you've got to throw all those rules out and download the upgrade as fast as you can. Kids change. Lord, do they change—and fast.

You can tuck your little dimple-cheeked sweetheart into bed one evening only to wake up to a complete stranger the next morning. The kid has shot up four inches overnight and is suddenly using your razor. His frontal lobe has expanded and he's thinking about stuff you haven't boned up on. He's reading Kafka and you're sitting there with *Goodnight Moon* in your hand. There are times when I feel like I'm so out of it that I'll have to sprint just to reach stupid. Parenting is like that nightmare where you're suddenly in the wrong classroom, at someone else's desk, staring at a test you haven't studied for.

And you can't sit still as a parent. You do so at your own peril, believe me. You have to stay alert, stay on your feet, watch them like hawks and listen as though your life (and theirs) depended on it. Even then, understand that you will miss stuff. You will miss little clues, little telltale signs of trouble or change or upheaval. Guaranteed, you will drop the ball on occasion. And then, of course, you will kick yourself for being so blind. All parents are cursed with 20/20 hindsight.

Parenting is humbling. There are times when the enormity of the responsibility upon my shoulders just about paralyses me. Times when I think "Who in their right mind gave me this beautiful child to ruin."

We flounder, we flop, we reach spastically out to one another. We do our best. And hopefully, through the grace of God, we don't mess them up too badly. And we love them. Thank God we love them. Not because of anything they do to test us or try our patience but simply because sometimes, in some ridiculously complicated situations, love is all we have to offer. It's the only tool in what is very often a pathetically empty drawer.

I don't know, I don't understand, I don't remember—but I do love you. Thank God indeed. I'm hoping against hope that Lennon was right when he said, "all you need is love" because more and more I'm convinced, as the speed of this parenting race gets ratcheted up, that love is the only real credential I've got.

In the final analysis, all the wisdom, all the advice, all the instruction, all the experience—all of it—is piled precariously on one small, sturdy, scuffed-up little item called love.

ONCE YOU'RE CARDED,
THEY KNOW EVERYTHING!

For the first and probably the last time in their lives, my children were excited about going to the bank.

They had just opened up their first savings accounts; a momentous occasion to be sure. They felt grown-up, worldly and brimming with anticipation of a riches-filled future. As they should. That's what kids do best.

I confess to a slightly less optimistic sentiment. All I could think of was, "Well, they're on the radar screen now." The system had them. Prior to getting a hold of that little plastic card and signing those papers, they were as free as they were ever going to be in this world. They weren't on anybody's mailing list yet, they weren't in any database of potential customers, they were just a couple of *tabula rasas*—so to speak.

Oh sure, the government knew about them. They had health cards and birth certificates and social security numbers. They were by no means invisible to Big Brother. But still, those things are fairly benign. The government doesn't call you at home to see if you want to support the newest budget. The Ministry of Health doesn't cram your mailbox full of offers for better, platinum health cards. The birth certificate registry doesn't pester you to donate because you're an alumnus.

But, once you have money—once you *officially* have money—the sharks begin to circle. And that debit card that my kids think is so incredibly cool might as well be a financial chum-bucket.

The other, more worrisome side of it is that from this point on, as they grow older and acquire more and more cards for this and that, they will be studied and tracked and analyzed as though they were fugitives.

Information is digital gold in this brave new world. With every swipe we are sending a very eager someone all kinds of data about who we are, where we are going, what we are doing when we get there and what time of day we are doing it.

I had a glimpse into the machinations of the data collection world not long ago. Out of the blue one of my credit card companies called me and a very concerned voice said "Mr. Crone have you lost or replaced a credit card recently?"

"No," I replied warily.

"Well, Mr. Crone, this is just a precautionary call. We've noticed that lately you've been purchasing more bottled water than usual."

"Well, I…"

"And yet, when we cross-reference our database with your household water consumption, you don't appear to be using the toilet any more than usual which leads us to the conclusion that you may be retaining water."

"Huh…"

"I see also that you've purchased less music and more razor blades in the past month…this is a disturbing pattern Mr. Crone…Mr. Crone? Are you all right, Mr. Crone? Mr. Crone, if you'd like to talk to someone about the unhappiness in your life we have an excellent in-house psychiatrist who takes Interac. Mr. Crone, there's no need to feel despondent. A better life is only a swipe away."

"Swipe this."

Click.

We Owe Our Elderly Respect, Kindness

I'm not the first person to note the cruel irony that as humans get older we start to look more and more like we did when we first came into this world.

We lose our hair, we get chubby and wrinkly, we have a hard time walking. In certain cases we become as myopic as newborns, barely able to focus on things more than a few inches from our noses. Some of us even wind up wearing diapers again. Not much fun.

Yet all of this would be so much more tolerable if, as we were physically morphing back into toddlers, we were also given back the magical mindset of a child.

Wouldn't it be nice, after years of looking out at the world through the jaded eyes of an adult, to suddenly fall back in love with the wonder of it all through the sparkling peepers of a newborn?

Granted, going over to Grampa's house and finding him lying on his back, gurgling and happily playing with his toes might take a little adjustment. But it's one I would joyfully make if I believed my mom or dad was really and truly having a ball inside that 90-year-old body. And anyway, isn't that a much nicer scenario than having him staring hopelessly at a wall in some overcrowded, understaffed seniors' home?

I wish it were that way and I have to believe in my heart of hearts that it still can be that way. I'm not talking about aging into a coo-ing, helpless-if-happy lump, but, of hanging onto that wonder—or at least rediscovering it.

Part of the difficulty has to do with how the rest of us treat the aged. There doesn't seem to be as much reverence around as there used to be. I may be blowing smoke here, but it seems like in the old days our elders were treated with more respect. They were considered sages, keepers of ritual and traditional wisdom.

They played an integral part in what were often life and death decisions. Seriously, I've watched a lot of westerns and I've never ever seen Apache elders being shipped off to a seniors' teepee. My point is that if you tell someone often enough that they're no longer useful, pretty soon they'll start to believe it. Conversely, if you accord them respect and dignity and listen to and value their input, pretty soon they start dispensing real wisdom. I believe that.

I've long been an advocate of the power of the human spirit to literally create the world we experience. We do it. We are Dorothy's man behind the curtain, thinking into existence the wonders and horrors of this Oz we live in. No one and nothing else is responsible for what shows up in our lives, our societies, our cultures. If our lives become like pyramids, getting narrower and narrower as we age, then we have made them so. If our seniors and aged have given up hope, appear useless, outdated and burdensome, it is because we have told them they are, again and again and again in a thousand different and pointed ways.

Should I be given the gift of growing old, I should like to do so in grace and wonder. I can take the first steps to insuring that by revering and listening to my elders today.

River Gets Best of This Canoeist

Nothing pulls your pants down and spanks you like Mother Nature. Suzanne and I were hell-bent on getting into the canoes early this year. We wanted to be on the water before the bugs hatched and, more importantly, before the portaging started. I'm a lazy canoeist. If there's any way to avoid humping a canoe over ground, I'm for it. Last weekend, that laziness was my undoing.

We've paddled the Gibson dozens of times. But, as Heraclitus said, "You can never set foot in the same river twice." I've known the Gibson to be a placid senior, a playful child, even a rambunctious, unpredictable teenager. But this time around it was a like a pregnant woman in her 42nd week—angry, swollen and looking to beat on somebody.

We heard the rapids long before we saw them. That thunderous rumbling always sets my pulse racing. I am no courier de bois. I am more of a *coward* de bois. I have a healthy respect for white water. And when we pulled over to shore, got out and eyeballed this particular chute, I very clearly heard my sphincter shouting "Run Away!" This was serious water—an obsidian V slashing down into vicious, roiling haystacks and standing waves.

There was no thought of going anywhere near this monster with bodies in the boats. All evidence pointed to a portage. But the fat, lazy guy in the back of my head has a loud voice. Even above the jet engine roar of the rapids I could hear him whining, "A portage will take forever! Line the boats through!" And I did my first dumb thing of the day. I listened to him. We emptied the first canoe of its contents, and, with Suzanne on the stern and me on the bowline, began to release the hapless craft into the grip of the current. Things went well for about five seconds. Then all hell broke loose.

In a flash the stern was swallowed by a huge wave and the boat filled with green-gold water, no longer bobbing along the surface but snatched out of our control by several thousand tons of angry river.

All I could think of was if we try to hold onto it the water will bend it in half, so I did my second dumb thing of the day, I shouted "Let go of the rope!"

Suzanne did, and the two of us watched in horror as one of our ways home shot speedily down river. Then things really got goofy. I sped off down the riverbank in an insane effort to rescue the boat. My heart jackhammered through my life jacket as I flailed through brambles, skidded down lichen-covered boulders and came within inches of stepping on a huge Massassauga Rattler who, thank God, had the sense to get out of the way of the frenzied, wheezing nut-job thrashing his way through the bush.

Finally, there it was, 10 feet off shore and waving "Sayonara Stupid."

For the first time that day I did a smart thing. I didn't hesitate. I jumped into the frigid water and grabbed the stern rope.

Hours later, as we left Mother Nature's classroom and loaded the boats atop the van, I began to laugh uncontrollably.

I closed my eyes and took in huge gulps of fresh river air. We were all still here; still safe and, I hope, the wiser for our adventure.

I heard the far off rumble of the rapids, and it may have been my exhausted imagination, but just for a moment, it sounded like soft, female laughter.

WE GUYS LOVE DOING WHOLE LOT OF NOTHING

There is a beautiful simplicity to men that, I know a lot of the time, greatly exasperates women. But I cannot help but wonder if, at other times, they don't envy it just a little. I am the first to admit that of the two genders women are the better model—the upgrade, if you will. One need only read Genesis for evidence of this. God made man, the beta version, then got most of the bugs out and created woman. If women are the flexibility and intuitive efficiency of the newest computer operating system, then men are the simplicity and predictability of good old DOS.

If women are "The Goldberg Variations," men are "Happy Birthday to You."

If women are *The Iliad*, men are *There Once Was a Man From Nantucket...*"

Women seem to me more complex, more adaptable, more evolved even than men. But there is a wonderfully comfortable, out-of-the-box readiness that men seem to have that women, for all of there splendour, do not. Getting to know a woman can take a lot of work. You can get a handle on most men inside a six-pack. I may be wrong, but I think a lot women see this ease of access that men share and they secretly long for it.

This past weekend I went up to a cottage with a couple of buddies. And from the very first emailed communication this trip had the fundamental stamp of Cro-Magnon austerity about it. "Come to cottage. Chop down tree. Will get food and beer somewhere."

Twelve words and everything I needed to know. And that was as complicated as the weekend ever got.

In fact, if anything, the longer we spent together, alone without any exposure to or influence from females, the simpler we became. Given enough time, red meat and fermented grains, a visitor to that island would've found only three single-celled organisms sitting on the deck talking about the hottest mitochondria they ever shared osmosis with. That's just the way it goes with men. And that's precisely why we need women in our lives. The future of the species depends upon it.

But over a couple of days, a man can only devolve so far and it's a devolution into a very soothing place. We very quickly dispensed with the obligatory chainsawing and stacking of wood and embarked upon the real work of the weekend—eating, drinking and talking. Although, in fact, we never lit one, it seemed to me that the three of us were squatting around a fire all weekend, spears in hand, sometimes telling a story, sometimes listening, very often just staring into the flames.

That may be the biggest surprise of all to our female counterparts. How much men value and embrace silence on these trips. After a while an eerie sixth sense settles over everyone. Men have been known to get up, get their mates a beer and sit down again, all without a word. It's quite something.

When men return home from such get-togethers, they are invariably asked the same question "What did you guys do all weekend?" And just as invariably, they give the same answer "Nothing."

As exasperating and unfathomable as that response must be to a woman, it is the golden, simple, secret truth.

There Are Some Really Tough Gigs in This World.

I was out driving the other day and I found myself having to slow down for a couple of crows trying to make a meal of a freshly squashed skunk. Imagine being a crow. Not only is your diet chiefly comprised of stinking, maggot-infested dead stuff, but just to even get to the bloated, rotting entree, you have to dodge thousand-pound vehicles moving at more than 100 km/hr. Sound good? Anybody want to sign up for that one? Suddenly my commute isn't looking so bad.

Or maybe you'd like to be a cardinal? On the surface being a cardinal seems like a lot of fun. They get to fly, they have a beautiful song. Who doesn't like cardinals? But there comes a moment in every cardinal's life when he realizes just how badly he's been screwed.

That moment comes the first time he leans over a pond or a lake for a drink of water and sees his reflection.

"Oh crap! I'm red!"

And not just any red—bright red.

Not rust or russet or anything that might remotely be construed as camouflage—just dazzling, target red.

Every hawk, owl and cat for miles thinks he's won the lottery when Mr. Cardinal wings his merry way into the neighborhood.

Hell, there are legally blind cats that can still take down a cardinal. There are hawks with cataracts, owls plagued with conjunctivitis who are still alive, solely because of the suicidal plumage of the cardinal.

Then, as if being the take out of the cat world wasn't bad enough, they don't get to go south in the winter. That, apparently, would make far too much sense. South, after all, is where other bright red things live and grow. Things that might provide a smidgen of safety for an exhausted red bird.

No, instead, let's stay up north where our intense red will be notched up to neon against the white of snow. Good call. Wouldn't you love to be a fly on the wall of some cardinal nest when their teenage son, whose loon and oriole pals are all packing up for the family trip to Florida, finds out he's staying put?

"Daaaaaad! Don't you get it? We're red! Oh man, this is so messed up."

"Son, I know you don't like it, but we have to stay here."

"Um, hello? Earth to Dad…wings? We can go anywhere we want!"

"Son, don't speak like that to your father."

"Oh, shut up Mom, you're not even really red."

Yep, that's a parenting nightmare.

Still, cardinals seem pretty happy. Crows too, for that matter. Most creatures actually, outside humans, seem very content with their lot in life. You'll never hear a word of complaint from the ant or the bee or the dung beetle. Even the lowly mosquito who sometimes lives for less than a week, manages to pack a lot of living into those seven days.

We, at the top of the food chain, with the sweetest gig of all, seem to be the only ones complaining. Think about that. And, next time you're reaming some poor waitress because your steak is overdone, think about that crow with his beak two feet up a dead skunk's butt.

Perspective is everything.

Gazebo Adventure a Nightmare

Throughout history the gods have saved especially delicious forms of penance for those who dare to walk amongst them. Icarus had his wings melted for daring to fly too close to the sun. Medusa ended up with a seriously bad hair day for loving herself too much and have you seen Joan Rivers lately?

I'm still unsure what I did to deserve it, but my particular atonement was called *The Gazebo of Devilment*.

I suppose I should have paid more heed to the salesperson's warning that "these babies can be a little tricky to put up." But I didn't. Nor did I give much weight to the fresh bandages on his fingers or the nervous tick around his left eye.

In my hubris, I saw only a few quick turns of an Allen key and then me, drink in hand, underneath my new outdoor shelter. I smugly drove the thing home, dragged it onto the back deck and naively slit open the box, which clearly should have been marked "Pandora."

For starters, the instruction booklet was nowhere to be found. Understand, I am a big instructions guy. I take great comfort from clearly numbered sequences and detailed procedures. There is no such thing in my world as too simple a direction. My ideal instruction manual has chapter headings like "Getting to know your screwdriver," "What is a nail?" and "Time to call Dad." There was no such animal in this crate. In fact, after frantic minutes of digging through assorted hardware and tearing open bags of screws and bolts I found one tiny sheet, a microfiche really, with a faded diagram on it. *The Dead Sea Scrolls* were more legible.

Still, like Sisyphus, the Donner party or Tony Danza for that matter, I didn't know when to quit. My pride pushed me closer to oblivion. I began to haul everything out, anxiously flinging metal pieces of every imaginable size and shape all around me. Within minutes the deck looked like Juno Beach—and was every bit as dangerous.

Like an idiot I kept referring back to the hieroglyphic instruction napkin, as though any kind of salvation lay in that postage stamp of misinformation. I may as well have been flipping through *Cosmo* for all of the practical use it was. At least with *Cosmo* I might have finally found my G spot or learned how to turn a woman on. No such luck with this project.

Soon my wife joined me and inside of two washers and a self-tapping screw our matrimonial bonds were straining like a strapless bra on Pamela Anderson. Then the kids appeared just in time to learn a few new choice words—all of which rhymed in one way or another with Nantucket.

Then, slowly, strut by twisted strut, bracket by bent bracket, the monstrosity took shape. But nothing was as it should've been and every pyrrhic victory was countered by a thousand wrong angles and mismatched joints.

The thing looked less like a gazebo than a piece of modern art or possibly a downed aircraft.

Finally, broken and exhausted, I found myself prostrate at the altar of duct tape…the last hope for the truly perplexed. Several hours later, their punishment wrought, the gods left me alone. Well, not entirely. I have, on my back deck, a misshapen, leaning reminder of my own fallibility.

Becoming the Men We Always Wanted To Be

It's funny the things that become important to us as we grow older—the things we feel it necessary to hold on to. When my grandmother died some years ago, the only thing I really wanted from a houseful of objects was a cracked, butter-yellow ceramic ewer. An ordinary item made priceless to me because it was the vessel she'd always used to serve us hot chocolate.

I have the collars of every dog I have owned and loved. I can't bring myself to throw them out or give them away. I have my grandfather's WW I uniform. And lately, I have noticed that I am collecting more and more of my father's paraphernalia. This is, no doubt, a function of two separate phenomena: a) he is getting older and naturally divesting himself of what he considers junk and b) he is getting older and I am hanging onto every piece of him that I can get.

My dad hasn't smoked in decades, but I have his old Zippo lighter. I have a drawer full of his old pocket and hunting knives. With the recent departure of the cottage I have inherited a garage full of my dad's tools and hardware. I have his trophy muskellunge mounted in my parlour. I think I know why I do this; why I keep all of these things. They are—all of them—talismans and touchstones that seem to keep him with me, both emotionally and physically. Superstitious? Silly? Maybe, but this is powerful magic and I'm not about to mess with it. You don't throw your dad's stuff out while he's still around.

I'm naturally curious as to what stuff of mine my own children will glom onto. What pieces of me will seem to radiate most strongly with my dad-ness? My keyboard? My glasses? Maybe my canoe paddle? Who am I kidding? It'll probably be the whoopee cushion and the fart machine.

It's odd that this process doesn't seem to apply to my mother's possessions. Maybe it's strictly a gender issue, but I tend to keep my mother's flame deep inside me. With my dad I like a more tangible reminder. And so I happily store away his things. I have no desire, for instance, to hang onto my mom's apron or sewing kit or even the wooden spoon she used to whack us with (although it seems to me that item should have a hallowed place somewhere.) I suspect that my mom's memory will be preserved much in the same way that my grandmother's is. There will be one special article, one key that will most easily open the doors of memory. Maybe that wooden spoon will resurface after all.

But with dads and their sons, it is different. Perhaps the answer lies in the fact that most of us spend a lifetime trying to be like our fathers. And with every little acquisition, every tool, knife, lighter and trophy fish, we feel that we are that much closer to being the man we always wanted to be.

Why Do So Many of Us Prefer the Past to the Future?

It's funny, but if you ask little children where they would like to go if they could time travel, most of them will say the future. Pose the same question to most adults and they're likely to say somewhere in the past. Why is that?

I am a person who firmly believes that we are getting better, albeit very slowly, as a species. But I too, if I'm being honest, would have to answer that I'd like to go back in time. The future, for some reason, doesn't excite me that much.

It seems that at some point in most of our lives something changes. Our optimism fades. Maybe it's simply that as we grow and take on more responsibility and worry and stress, the simpler world of our childhood becomes more appealing.

In my romantic naivete, I find myself longing to live back in the days when an individual could still opt out of society if he or she chose to—when there were still unknown frontiers in this world and a person could freely live in a place where fresh air, clean water and nutritious food were in abundance. The irony is that the future I hope for will include all of those things and more. And the frontiers will exist on other planets, other galaxies.

But the future, for all the faith I may put in it, is still a question mark. The past is tangible. I know that if I go back to Ontario in the early 19th century I will find homesteads and horses and hard work. I will also, of course, find influenza, polio and rampant infant mortality. I might very well be a few inches shorter too, gout-riddled and, in all likelihood, dead at my current age of 46. Cripes, there's always a catch, isn't there?

I think that catch, though, is where the truth lies. When I think of living in the past I do so because I yearn for peace, simplicity and a slower, more meaningful lifestyle. All of these things can be mine in the year 2006, if I am, like the 19th century pioneer, willing to work at them. And, just like his farm was the fruit of his labours, my community, my city, my country, my world can now be the fruit of mine. The horse and the plough and the bucksaw have been replaced by the Internet, the silicon chip and digital technology. What kind of crops do we want to sow? What kind of a future do we want?

I, with my computer and fax and cell phone, have more power than ever before in the history of mankind to meaningfully shape the world around me. Science and medicine have allowed me to live twice as long as I might have a mere 100 years ago—twice as much opportunity to make things better.

Perhaps the main reason that so many of us prefer the past to the future is that we wrongfully feel that the future is a mystery that we have no control over. But if we don't decide what our future will bring, who will?

IT'S TIME TO UPDATE
ANNIVERSARY MARKERS

My wife and I are about to celebrate our 20th wedding anniversary. Technically, it's the china anniversary. Somehow that doesn't seem appropriate. China implies fragility, even a propensity to shatter. I'm proud of the fact that my partner and I have hung in for two decades, two kids, three houses, four cats and five dogs.

No, china doesn't cut it. I think 20 years should be the plywood anniversary. Plywood is strong, yet it also has a lot of give. This flexibility allows it to maintain its integrity under enormous pressure. If you look at plywood carefully you'll see that it is not constructed of one piece of wood, but of many different pieces glued together—the sum having greater strength than the parts. Plywood also swells and retains water as it gets older. Could one find a more apt symbol for marriage?

Now, I realize that no union is bulletproof. There's no guarantee that Suzanne and I will still be an item in another 20 years. Indeed, if those photos from my junket to Thailand ever hit the Internet I doubt I'd give us another 20 minutes. So, in light of that and in light of the state of matrimony in general these days, perhaps we should update our anniversary markers.

What about the Briggs and Stratton anniversary, connoting a marriage that, like a powerful engine, relies on many different parts to function as an efficient whole but which, occasionally, mows somebody else's grass?

Or the Scotch anniversary—a marriage that started out neat but which is now clearly on the rocks?

The Filter Queen anniversary—35 years and it still sucks? The Keanu anniversary—a marriage of two physically gorgeous people that, although void of any substance or intellect, is still, inexplicably, successful? The Snap-on anniversary—a marriage where the participants are clearly both tools, but they work beautifully together? The parsley anniversary—where both partners are still interested in the main course, but they like a little on the side? And, finally, the hay anniversary—where you're both still on the same tractor but one of you is thinking of baling?

Another consideration is how to mark this anniversary. We had discussed an exotic trip or perhaps an expensive night out in the city, but I think we've finally come to the perfect solution—a new bed. Romantic dinners and strolls along the beach are all well and good, but after 20 years I can tell you that the bed is where a marriage is made or broken. And I'm not just talking about the obvious. Physical intimacy, while important, can only take a marriage so far (although I'm certainly willing to see just how far that might be). But that bed is where, not only your bodies, but your spirits link. Where you lie in the dark and listen to your children sleeping. Where you quietly talk about money and fears and dreams and the future. Where you listen to storms pounding on the windows and where you watch the sun rise on a new day. Where, as bad as things might get, you are never alone.

OLD-TIMER'S BIRTHDAY PARTY
A REAL GEM

I went to my Uncle Jack's 80th birthday party yesterday. I really like my Uncle Jack. Every kid should have an Uncle Jack.

My Uncle Jack builds his own canoes, has thick white hair and hands like a catcher's mitt.

Throughout his 80 years he has fished and hunted and had an abiding love of dogs, poker, fresh berries and ice cream.

How can you not love a guy like that?

As a young boy, and even now, I never tired of hearing the story (perhaps apocryphal—frankly I don't care) of how my Uncle Jack thumped out his bully of a gym teacher. You need to be an Uncle Jack to do that. Uncle Irvings don't thump out their gym teachers.

I've always had a soft spot for my Uncle Jack.

We spent Jack's birthday cruising around his favourite spot, Stoney Lake, where his family has islanded for generations. It was, aside from Captain Grumpy Pants' Bly-like barking of the onboard rules and regs, quite wonderful. This clown had me shaking my head. He was like Captain Stubing with a bad case of piles. It's a birthday party for an 80-year-old gentleman for crying out loud and this guy sounds like he's addressing a room full of drunken coeds. Hey, Commodore, I dig the white socks but it's a cruise boat, not the freaking *Bismarck*.

I made eye contact with my brothers and it was plain we were all thinking the same thing.

"Let's pants this stiff and toss him overboard. How hard can it be to steer this thing?"

Anyway, once Admiral Halsey finished dressing us down, it was a lot of fun. And, as well as a birthday party, it turned out to be a sizeable family reunion. The boat was so full of relatives on my dad's side that, had the *Chippewa II* gone down, our DNA would've disappeared from the planet.

I saw aunts and cousins and second cousins I've not seen for years. Some I met for the first time. I took great delight from sitting in the sun, beer in hand, the stunning, granite-studded topography rolling slowly by, and just watching everyone.

I was immediately struck by how much older we all are and yet, how very much the same we have remained. I noticed my brothers and sister laughing loudly over a shared joke with some cousins and an aunt and I realized the laughter and the eyes of everyone in that circle were exactly the same as those found around our extended family's Christmas table 30-odd years ago. We're like diapers in that sense—it's what's inside that counts. That never changes.

Finally, and most importantly, I witnessed a quiet conversation between my dad and my Uncle Jack. They were standing along the railing of the boat, each gesturing in turn at some bay or shoal or patch of lily pads that they had fished together over the last six decades. I saw them then as the wispy-haired octogenarians they had become, but also as the boyhood friends they had been, tanned and fit and paddling these waters in a canoe. And I wondered what it felt like for them. To be there together, to look back, to smile silently and comfortably in the presence of a lifelong friend. If it made them feel half as good as it did me, Jack couldn't have asked for a better birthday present.

Like a poor actor missing his cue, bad news often enters our lives at the most inappropriate and sometimes brutally ironic moments. His clumsiness, in fact, is so chronic I cannot recall one case from my life when bad news was ever timely.

Yesterday I had just sent my boys and one of their pals off into the playful surf of a Georgian Bay beach, and was, in fact, about to join them, when my cellphone rang. I picked it up, embarrassed and feeling very much the idiot—and realizing as well that I had suddenly become one of those people I disdain; individuals who cannot get away from their phones.

I said, "Hello" and watching my children diving, laughing and glorying in the sun and the emerald water, heard my wife's heartbroken voice tell me that her brother's son, our 16-year-old nephew, Francis, had died in his sleep that night.

All around me people chuckled and chatted and played. Children shrieked and splashed, chased one another in and out of the waves.

My own sons beckoned to me impatiently, treading in the deep, smiling brilliantly and shaking the water from their hair as the breakers rolled over them. And yet, here was this car wreck in my ear, this poison, this damp, cold drizzle from a thousand miles away. The contrast was almost comical—almost.

I did not tell my children what had happened then, opting instead to let them enjoy their day, to let me enjoy them, be healed by them. Still, try as we might, we adults are never fully able to enter back into the joyous oblivion of childhood and throughout the fun of that afternoon I found myself coming back again and again to my sweet nephew and the necessary, soul-wrenching anguish of my brother-in-law and his wife.

In a bittersweet irony, every time I touched one of my boys, every time I saw that magnificent light in their eyes and the sun glistening on their tanned and perfect bodies, I was reminded that these things were now all past tense for John and Mary and Francis. What a strange and complex emotional stew I was swimming in. So saddened and heartbroken and yet so blissfully glad to be here, to be alive, to be a father to living, breathing, noisy kids.

I did take one consolation from that strange afternoon so full of contrasts. My nephew, challenged from birth with severe cerebral palsy among a litany of other ailments, was now, at least in my own theology, free.

As I sat on the beach, one protective eye on my own babies, I imagined Francis's spirit already reborn in some perfect, poetic incarnation. I saw him as one of the gulls circling so easily and beautifully in that brilliant sky, or perhaps one of the millions of silvery fish in those crystalline waters, darting and leaping athletically at will or maybe simply as the warm August wind, now dancing and swirling ecstatically around and about the sun-dappled shoulders of my children, his cousins.

Be a man and run those rapids

There are a number of things that go through your head as you are capsizing a canoe into a series of rapids with your 11-year-old son in the bow.

"Oh my goodness! Whose idea was this?"

"You are a very stupid man."

"Is anyone looking?"

I've canoed for many years, kayaked for just as many. But yesterday was the first time I have ever upset a boat in whitewater—the first *accidental* wetting in 20 years.

I used to be proud of my dry record, but in light of my recent baptism I'm rethinking things. I now realize I have been, not to put too fine a point on it, a scaredy paddler, a water wussy.

One of the many wonderful things about having children is they often force you to become a better version of yourself. When we are youngsters we strive hard to better ourselves in order to impress our parents, to gain their favour, their attention, their love.

Next, when we are entering relationships, there may be short periods where we are striving to better ourselves in order to impress a prospective life mate. But then, after we are settled down in our lives with our partners, many times there comes a doldrum of sorts. We are on a kind of growth cruise control. We may feel like we've made enough progress. We coast. That is, until children come along. Once more we have someone to strive for, someone to impress, someone to be better for. Like it or not, we become role models.

And so, yesterday, as we pulled over to the safety of the portage entrance, a little voice in the back of my head began to speak up. I've heard this voice many times before. In the past he has said such things to me as:

"Go on up. That ladder's not so high."

And "It's wiring…how hard can it be?"

This time he was saying only two words: "Run it." Run the rapids.

Run it. Never have two words been so pregnant with meaning. Run the rapids. Show your son you are not afraid. Show him how not to be afraid. Show him how to live. Show yourself. Amen.

The opinions of certain film directors notwithstanding, I am not an idiot. My innate sense of caution has served me well in the past. I have all my limbs and digits to prove it.

But when you are getting back into your canoe and paddling upstream to retake a heading on a dark V of ominously rushing water and your son turns to you from the bow, looks at you with the eyes of your own childhood and lays his soul in your hands with a trusting "I'm nervous Dad," you don't paddle for shore. Thanks to that blessing-in-a-baseball-cap, you suddenly find yourself with the strength of 10 Grinches plus two. A braver and better you than you were five minutes ago, you slash down into the white water.

Seconds and millennia later, as you bob to the surface amidst a sea of floating camp gear, eagerly clutching the hand of your smiling, still wonderfully trusting son, you may call out to him, "Are you all right, buddy?"

But what you are really saying is "Thank you son. Thank you."

You Just Have to Find That Wheeeeee!!! Moment

I have a favourite cartoon tacked up in my office. In it a man is standing behind his young daughter as she sits on a swing. About to pull her back for her first ride, he offers this advice "You can say anything you want, or you can say nothing, but most people say 'Wheeeeee!!!'"

I like that philosophy. I make it a point to try and find something to say "Wheeeee!!!" about every day, even if it means walking over to the school and trying out the swing for a while. Some days, of course, are harder than others to find a "Wheeee!!!" moment in.

Those days when my bank balance looks more like binary code than a financial statement, when my credit card bill has to be delivered on a flatbed and when it seems that the last time my agent called me I had a rotary phone.

Still, thankfully, even during my bleakest periods there is usually something to "Wheeee!!!" over—watching my wife get dressed, the smell of coffee, a dog's head in my lap, an unlooked for and voluntary hug from a child, cold chocolate milk, cookies, watching my wife get undressed.

In fact, a good thing to do on those apocalyptic days—days when Job wouldn't trade gigs with you—is to sit quietly somewhere and do a little blessing inventory. This can be difficult at first, but stay with it and I guarantee, with a little patience, good stuff will start occurring to you. Even when I was laid out with cancer, my tired veins crammed full of chemicals you wouldn't spray on a cockroach, I still had the breeze on my face and the dancing shadows of the leaves on the carpet.

I had books and stories and when my eyes grew too tired to read I had music and when even my ears grew weary, I had silence. There is always something.

Some people call this the art of appreciation, some call it perspective. I have started calling it "Looking for the Wheeee!!!" And I've come to realize how essential it is to not only endure, but enjoy our time here.

There's much more philosophy in that little cartoon than meets the eye. As the father says to his little girl, "You can say anything you want, or you can say nothing."

The wonderful thing about being sentient is that we always have a choice. Is the glass half full or half empty? Are things getting better or worse? Do you want fries with that? How our lives turn out and what shows up in them has everything to do with how we feel about being here.

If we believe that life is a struggle, that it is something to be tolerated, that we are born into guilt and fear and strife, then that is what we will have.

But if we consider this world our playground and those people who come into our lives our playmates, then it seems to me we will enjoy the ride a heck of a lot more.

Climb on up into that swing and ask yourself, are you looking for the "Wheeee!!!" or are you stuck with the "Whoa!!!"?

NOTHIN' LIKE LIVIN' IN A SMALL TOWN

When you make your home in a small town there is a certain shorthand for living that one soon catches on to.

For instance, although I've been a resident of this lovely little hamlet for close to 15 years I really couldn't tell you, offhand, the names of any streets outside a block of my own home.

I doubt any of my neighbors could either. We've never learned them because we don't have to. Nobody really uses them. Frankly I don't know why the municipality even bothers to put up street signs. For instance, I don't live at 32 Bodrington—I live in the old Pendergrast place, kitty-corner to the Legion, right near where Arch Lumley got run over by the Santa Claus float. Much more helpful, don't you think, than 32 Bodrington? Certainly more colourful.

Likewise, there is a centuries-old method of giving directions in small towns. If you want to tell someone how to get to the diner, you don't blather on with a bunch of north and souths and avenue this or street that. Instead, you say "Get yerself to the main drag and follow Percy."

Everybody knows Percy pretty much lives at the diner. Follow him for a few minutes and he'll take you right there. He may swing you past the hardware store and Co-op first, but eventually, sure as shootin', you'll get to the diner. Anyway, who couldn't use a stop at the hardware store or the Co-op?

Names too, in a small town, have their own unique conventions. You can't just start in a conversation with something like "I heard the Snoddon boy's been at it again." Goodness, no. Do that and you're apt to start a feud that'd make the Hatfield and McCoy's look like a square dance.

Anybody with a brain knows that there are more Snoddons in town than there are pickup trucks. Which one are you talking about? Same thing with Brethours and Purvis's and Teefys. And don't even get me started on the Dobles. This is what you get in a small town— families that have been around for hundreds of years. They are proud, upright, hardworking, pioneering stock and if you want them to help you slander somebody, you have to be more particular. Narrow it down. Walk your listeners in, step by step, until they know exactly who you're gossiping about.

Try this: "I heard that Snoddon boy, the one lives over to the Bagshaw place, kid with the wonky eye, old man has the gout so bad he rides a lawn tractor all over hell and gone, dead dog on the front lawn, been there for a month of Sundays, the brother put a sled through the ice three year ago…and the girl's an awful size…I heard he's at it again."

Now, instead of the evil eye, you'll get a table full of nodding base-ball caps. Everybody knows that kid. And everybody will know exactly what "it" is that he's been at again without further explanation. It's a remarkably efficient system. One that, if you live in a small community, is well worth learning. Trust me. I'm the writer in town. Not the good one, the one with the pretty wife, not a brain in his head but a helluva dancer, wide fella, walks like he's got a load in his pants.

I Just Can't Resist Doing a Project

I had no idea I was a raving control freak until my children began asking me for help with their school assignments. I have a difficult time, apparently, simply giving advice or steering their little minds toward the right resources. Stemming from God knows what personal dysfunctionality, I have a desperate need to run the show. Perhaps it's my vocation. As an actor and a writer I have a great deal of autonomy in how I deal with things. Creative choices, especially, are almost always made by me and me alone. And so I sometimes have an issue or two regarding sharing the canvas.

It is not enough, for instance, to suggest that my son do a colourful title page for his assignment about frogs. No—I must comb the Internet, download pages of data and photographs. I join an Amphibian Chat room as Vic—blond, fit, into NASCAR, Metallica and wetlands conservation. I meet and blatantly flirt with Doris, a leopard frog enthusiast who digs guys in hip waders. I unashamedly lead her on, shyly and painfully recounting the tale of my divorce from a shrew with issues regarding my many pairs of hip waders in the bedroom. Smitten, the unwitting Doris happily sends me frog pictures from her private collection. Bingo—I'm in. The other kids won't have anything like this, I chuckle, finishing the download and blowing the hapless Doris off with a click of the mouse. Cruel, unfeeling? Yes, I know, but we're talking about my project here. Well, OK, my *son's* project, but still, if something's worth doing, it's worth doing right. Right?

At this point, while shocked and perhaps a little embarrassed by the previous display, my son is nonetheless happy to have the assignment completed. He is about to head off for some idle recreation with a pal when I point out to him that we may not be the only ones in class handing in an assignment with glossy photos.

Anybody can get pictures. We need audio. For a few mad seconds I actually consider chucking the whole paper parcel and going multimedia. I picture the teacher, no, the entire staff, beaming from the back of the class as slide after fantastic slide glimmers its way onto the screen, accompanied by the ideal musical score.

Handel's "Water Music" perhaps, or maybe Ravel's "Bolero" as a sexy counterpoint to pond scum. But…I am overdoing it—getting carried away.

I laugh and my son laughs too, if not a little too loudly, and is once again about to head out the door when I collar him.

"Costumes!" I blurt. I'll bet none of the other kids will be delivering their presentations dressed as frogs.

Once again I am at the computer, clicking and dragging my way through wholesale green felt distributors. I google Jim Henson. I am searching for tape measure, chalk and pinking shears when I hear a noise from behind me.

It is a noise I have heard before, one that I am familiar with and not a little afraid of. It is my wife. I turn around and she is there, one hand on hip, the other wrapped protectively around our son. The two of them shake their heads and trot into the kitchen to eat cookies and happily redo the assignment.

I trudge to bed, haunted by their laughter. The next morning there are 50 emails from someone named Doris.

WE ARE SIMPLY INSURED TO DEATH

It occurred to me the other day, as I was handing over my first-born child to a smiling man in glasses, how cripplingly insured I am. I have insurance for my car, my home, my mortgage, my finances, my health, my spouse's health, my children's health, my teeth, my family's teeth and probably the dog's teeth. I may even have insurance on my insurance.

I've no way of telling any more, it's all gotten so out of hand. I could have much more insurance too, if I could afford it. These days you can insure virtually anything. And you're encouraged to.

Pregnant? Worried the kid will have your father-in-law's taxi-cab ears? No sweat. If you've got the cash, we've got the policy.

One of my personal favourites is the extended warranty, where the same salesman who just spent 30 minutes convincing you that this computer is, without a doubt, the very finest, most reliable machine on the planet, now, as he rings up the sale, feels compelled to advise you to purchase a little $500 safety net—because you never can tell with these models.

We are the most insanely secure people to ever walk the earth. The flip side, of course, is that we are also the most fearful. We're terrified of everything.

We have had it drummed into our aching heads from birth that catastrophe, failure and financial ruin lurk just around every corner, that all of us are only a car ride or a Styrofoam cup of coffee away from permanent injury and that any child playing out of sight for more than

30 seconds may as well be on the back of a milk carton. Why don't we all just slash our wrists right now and be done with it?

The industry of fear is thriving. It's a good thing that, in 1893, Frederick Jackson Turner declared the North American frontier closed because, quite frankly, nobody can afford to go looking anymore.

The *Pinta,* the *Nina* and the *Santa Maria* never would've left the dock had they had existed today. Do you think Lewis and Clark stopped by Oregon Mutual before heading out across the continent just to cover their assets?

Do you suppose Magellan was granted the helm of the *Victoria* only as long as his 16-year-old son didn't drive? No. There was—there used to be—a thing called "risk." Attached to that thing called risk there were two other marvellous and now virtually extinct commodities—personal responsibility and courage. Back in the days when a kid could fall off his bike and his numb-nut parents wouldn't launch a class-action suit against the earth's gravitational field.

I'm not idiot enough to think that there is no merit in insurance. It has its place and God knows I've been helped by it on numerous occasions. But it's dawning on me that we have become a generation of wimps. People so pummelled and bruised by frightening headlines, sound bytes and unimaginably stupid court decisions that we are afraid to go outside our own homes without the condom of insurance wrapped firmly around us. A fitting garment considering how badly we've screwed things up.

There's Just No Answer to This Madness

It's a headline like something Quentin Tarentino's twisted melon might've dreamed up: "Insane Milkman Executes Amish Girls."

What are you supposed to do with a day that starts out with that news? Where do you go from there? How do you square that with whatever theology or philosophy gets you by?

What always goes through my mind in these cases is weren't there at least a few telltale signs? One or two things that maybe his wife or colleagues down at the dairy might've picked up on? Maybe taken him aside at lunch and asked him how things were going?

I could be talking through my hat here, of course. I'm no trained psychologist, but that question always bothers me.

I think it bugs me mostly because we don't generally, as a culture, tend to want to get involved anymore.

We have become very insular, squirrelled away in our living rooms, dens and home theatres. We have lost much of what used to be called a sense of community—something the Amish, ironically, still have a great deal of and treasure.

Somehow I don't think the Amish would let someone's mental illness get to the point where he needs to murder to exorcise his demons.

When was the last time you heard of a Mennonite serial killer? But the rest of us? Well, frankly, we just don't want to know, do we? If Ed, in accounting, sits at his desk and shreds one letter after another into a million tiny pieces of hate, that's just Ed. I'd talk to him about it but I gotta get home to catch *Survivor Keswick.* And besides, the guy creeps me out.

One of the great failings of the millennium is that very few of us really talk anymore. We have devices that will allow us to chat in our car with people on the other side of the globe. We can send and receive email in less time than it takes to dial a phone.

We have the greatest technical infrastructure the world has ever known. Yet not a lot of communication is going on. Of course, communication requires that not only does somebody talk, but that someone else has to listen. And listening requires slowing down, focusing, attending, being still. All of which seem to run counter to the rules of our Type A society.

I don't know a lot about the Amish. I don't necessarily agree with all the tenets of their faith.

I happen to be in love with and slavishly dependent on the electricity and technology that allows me to write these words while sitting out on my deck in the sunshine. I also think music and colour and diversity are things to be celebrated, not shunned.

Still, I think there are a number of pages the rest of us could take out of their book. We need to reacquaint ourselves with friends and family. We need to look after each other. We might not raise a barn together but we can make that handshake and hug last just a second or two longer. We can phone just for the hell of it. We can wave. We can turn the set off and walk outside. And we can talk. For the sake of those tiny, slain angels, please God, let us talk.

Wrong Notes Are Music to a Parent's Ears

My youngest brought his trombone home yesterday for the first time. As I sat downstairs in my office, futilely pounding away at the keys in my 30th attempt to rewrite the same thought, I was serenaded by what sounded like a diarrheal gorilla in the family room above me.

I just smiled. Over the years I have been accompanied in my various office pursuits by ragged piano scales, caterwauling electric guitars, the oom-pah-pah of a tuba and the artillery of a drum kit. I love them all—not so much the instruments or even the music. I just love the sound of a kid practising.

There are very few things that capture the essence of home and family better than the off-key strains of a child hacking away at a musical instrument. And this time of the year, walking around town, you can hear it floating discordantly from every second window. Dead birds litter the ground outside the house of a child with a new violin. Beaming, proud parents, blood running from their ears, sit out on porches while the next Gene Krupa flails away in the basement. A giant maple tree suddenly loses all of its leaves in one day outside the bedroom window of the new second clarinet. It's delightful.

Delightful because there is so much more than just music going on here. A child practising an instrument is infinitely more than just notes and chords. It's the sound of promise and potential. It's the sound of determination, discipline and obedience. It's the sound of a television or video game not turned on. And it's the glorious sound of "maybe."

Parents know the sound of "maybe" intimately. Our heads are ringing with the sound of "maybe" and "what if" and "who knows" the minute we hold our children—the instant we dream of a dazzling future for that tiny bundle of possibilities.

I wonder if our children might cut us a little more slack about practising or lay off the sulky scoliosis look at the keyboard if they realized this. If they understood that when we zealously encourage them to take up an instrument or when we nag and harp about sticking with it when it's patently obvious to everyone but us that the kid's hands are clearly meant to operate nothing more subtle than a backhoe, we are not purposely being overbearing idiots. We are merely worshipping at the altar of "maybe." That's the same altar heaped with mountains of hockey sticks and figure skates and ballet slippers, all in the name of love—misguided or otherwise.

I was visiting with friends the other day and they proudly pointed out the newest addition to their family—an upright piano. Not a new piano, but, in my opinion, all the more lovely for its wear and tear, its years of adolescent combat. It sat completely and immediately at home in their parlour, awaiting the next little bum to squirm impatiently on its stool, the next set of chubby, jam-stained fingers to stutter across its keys.

They told me when and where they bought it. They didn't have to tell me why. A day or two later, driving by their place, I saw the tiny silhouette of a little girl at the keyboard and through the open window came the halting, repetitive, breathtaking sound of "maybe."

Bellhop Gratuities Confound
Weary Traveller

Sometimes I feel like an idiot when I travel—like I'm two years old. The problem is, I think, that I don't travel enough. In fact, I travel just infrequently enough to be completely ignorant of the current customs in terms of gratuities and bellhop behaviour.

For starters, unless I'm staggering under the weight of enough supplies to outfit the Franklin expedition, I don't generally require, nor seek, assistance in carrying my bags. I'm a fairly big guy. I can handle it. But in a lot of these hotels the minute you get out of the taxi there's this emaciated guy standing there looking desperately hopeful that you'll throw him a bone by way of your briefcase or suit bag.

Maybe it's just me, but I'm always overcome by a paralyzing guilt that if I don't let this stiff do his thing, and consequently grease his palm, he's going to crawl home later that day and find an empty crutch in the corner where Tiny Tim used to sit. It'll be my fault that there's no plum pudding. I've tried the "It's OK…I've got it" routine a number of times, blowing past the bellwaif and heading to the elevators, but it's just not worth it. Not only do I always get the impression that the guy's going to do something nutty like leave a severed horse's head in my bed, but with one very practiced smirk, these guys can make you feel like you're the scum of the earth—like a Colombian drug dealer, like there you are, walking to the freaking elevator wearing shoes that cost more than this guy's yearly take-home, and you can't help a dude out?

Sometimes it's all I can do not to turn around and scream, "Yes, alright, I'm an actor! But I'm not a star. I'm 'Cop No. 4' for Pete's sake.

I'm 'Irate Man in Parking Lot.' I'm 'Red-faced Attendant.' And I have kids at home who are going through shoes like Imelda Marcos. I drive a 12-year-old minivan! My wife needs braces! And these stupid shoes are wardrobe!" But it's no good. They see you staying at a five-star hotel, they recognize your mug from television, however vaguely, and they make a beeline. You're gold. You're Burt Convey.

So now, I give in. "Sure you can hail me the taxi that I've seen sitting out front for the past hour." "Phew, thanks, that computer bag was killing me." "Oh, so that's how the TV remote works."

But giving in is not the end of my travails; in fact it's only the beginning—because, inevitably, when the guy is done with his ridiculously unnecessary labours, he will stand there awkwardly, while I, just as awkwardly, do Kumon calisthenics in my head trying to figure out what the appropriate tip should be. And, of course, I never get it right. I either totally burn the guy with whatever insultingly small, but handy, change is in my pocket at the time, or I do something stupid by flipping him $20 and trying to sound like a member of the Rat Pack, "There ya go, Scooter. Stay away from the broads, huh?"

The Rat Pack? I'm an idiot.

If You Love Them, Give Your Children a Poppy

You can learn an awful lot about people in a doughnut shop. You can almost break society down into pastry categories—that guy's a fritter, crusty on the outside, soft and gooey on the inside. The lady with the variety pack is indecisive as hell and the dude with the Hawaiian sprinkle definitely swings both ways. It's a fairly accurate system. Of course, I was sitting there with a bran muffin in front of me. What does that tell you?

But I also took note of something else. Like clockwork, I watched senior after senior walk in sporting a poppy on a lapel, shirt-front or windbreaker and just as predictably, I watched young person after young person walk in, sponsoring nothing more important than Nike, GAP or Metallica.

I find this sad and not a little alarming. Don't get me wrong. I'm not Mr. Mooney or Archie Bunker. I was young once too and I understand and appreciate that a large part of the beauty and magic of young people is their delightful obliviousness. They are so firmly wrapped up in today that they're hardly cognizant of yesterday and not thinking much of tomorrow. It's what makes them such interesting and unpredictable entities. This is wonderful and natural and I really wouldn't want to change a hair of it.

However, as parents, as adults, as people who have come to understand that this world we walk through is a living, breathing product of all that has gone on before us, good and bad, doesn't it behoove us to occasionally nudge our progeny towards some form of social conscience? Perhaps, at least, for this one week out of 52? Wouldn't it be nice, for instance, if at this time of the year, as we hugged and kissed our children out the door in the morning, that along with their lunch and their backpack and their toque, we also made sure they had their poppy?

It's a very little thing. A tiny thing really, but one that literally makes a world of difference. I've no real proof but I'd bet my bran muffin that Dutch children wear poppies as do Belgian children, French children and German children. Anybody who has had war in their backyard and shells dropped in their playgrounds understands why that poppy is at least as important as a toque or a backpack or even, dare I say it, one of a million multi-colored rubber wristbands.

"Lest we forget" are much more than three poetic words trotted out every November 11. They are a warning—dire counsel shouted soundlessly from the bleeding, pale-lipped mouths of millions of war dead.

And what we do forget, more often than not, is whom those war dead are speaking for. Not themselves, surely. No. They are speaking for our children, for the future. For if we should forget, if we lose tangible, tactile memory with the sacrifices of the past, we do so at our children's peril, for it is they, not us, who will fight the next war. So if you love them, stick a poppy on them. Lest we forget.

Do They Even Call It Shaving Anymore?

It's getting harder and harder these days to find any kind of meaningful rites of passage or ritual in our lives.

In olden times a young boy could look forward to his first rifle, or his first time sleeping alone on the range with the herd, or even his first nervous kiss as entry into manhood. In some southern states all three could happen in the same night, depending on how lonely the kid was.

But in this insular, overly protective era where it seems we are systematically removing any and all dangers and challenges from the paths of our offspring, how does a young boy know when he has become a man?

"Here son, I've been saving this for a day like today. I reckon you're man enough to have it."

"Gosh Pa! Your old Xbox controller!"

Doesn't quite cut it, does it? That's why I was more than a little excited and not a little proud the other day when I walked into a drug store to buy my oldest his first shaving kit. For all of society's modern neutering, shaving still survives as a passage into manhood.

I thought it would be a simple process, buying my son a razor and some blades. I couldn't have been more wrong. Have you looked at what passes for shaving supplies lately? NASA doesn't have that kind of technology. I wanted, both for nostalgia's sake and educational purposes, to start him off with something simple. You wouldn't, after all, put your newly permitted 16-year-old behind the wheel of a Ferrari

Testarossa. Of course not. Similarly, I was looking for one of the old single-bladed safety razors to cut his teeth on, so to speak. Teach the lad the basics. Immerse him in the rich lore of shaving history. Maybe share a few off-colour shaving stories. Do they have those?

But no. The manufacturers of men's toiletries seem no longer interested in the lore of shaving. They're not even really that interested, as far as I can tell, in providing a clean, close shave, though they take every inch of ad space to tell you so. What they are interested in, apparently, is getting you to fork over a handsome wad of cash every month or so for some ridiculous plastic gizmo while tossing your old plastic gizmo into the landfill.

So now, instead of a razor, young men stand in front of a mirror with a thing in their hand that sounds like it might be more at home in Wernher Von Braun's laboratory—Mach this and fuse that. Good grief. They have even, in their marketing delirium, managed to pull the lather so far over our eyes that we are buying a razor that vibrates.

What does it say about our generation when we can be induced to spend a fair chunk of change for the privilege of holding a shaky razor to our throats? And none of these, by the way, is a shaving kit. They are now shaving systems—no doubt tested at zero gravity.

At last, the best I could do that day was to come home with a dust-covered package containing a relic that held only three blades. Still, my son, bless him to pieces, couldn't have been happier. He's a good man.

Wonderful Burdens to Bear at This Time of Year

I was walking to the post office the other day and I bumped into my dear old friend Iris. Iris is, of course, not her real name. I'd like to use her real name, but it's too risky. Iris is, I'm pretty sure, a member of an inner council or a secret tribunal of seniors in this town—the grey-haired Illuminati who really hold the power around here.

Think I'm joking? From time to time in small towns like mine, people go missing. They're just *not there* one day. Everyone says "Oh, I guess Fred moved away" or "Well, I haven't seen Thelma in a while, she must be feeling poorly."

But they know what's really happened. We all know. Fred *went away* alright. He was run out of town on a rail after failing to hold the door to the Legion open for old Mrs. Norris. And Thelma's feeling a good deal worse than poorly, I can guarantee you that. Nobody makes old Wilf Suggins run his electric scooter off the sidewalk and onto the grass and lives to tell the tale. I don't care if she did have three kids in tow, and the youngest pitching a fit. That's Wilf Suggins, lady. The Grey Godfather.

I don't have any proof, but I'd bet a year's salary that the bottom of Lake Scugog is littered with the bodies of people unfortunate enough to cross the Council of Wrinkles—or whatever they're called. And every one of those bodies is wearing a cement cardigan, if you get my drift. So no, I don't even want to think of what might happen if I should inadvertently peeve Iris off. For starters it's a sure thing I'd never see a tray full of homemade Nanaimo bars again and my kids wouldn't be able to buy a snow shoveling job in this town.

So Iris and I got to gabbing. More accurately, Iris got to gabbing, I shut my mouth and minded my elders. I soon gathered that this is a big time of the year for grammas and great grammas like Iris. It's baking and knitting time—gearing up for Christmas time. Iris went on and on about how much work she had ahead of her. Oh, there were pans and pans of squares to lay up, enough booties to knit to outfit the Chinese army, and shortbread? My gaul, you'd have to haul it away in a truck. And of course there were the afghans. Talking with Iris, I began to realize that, more than just a comfortable something to toss around your shoulders or throw over your lap on a cold day, afghans are actually a unit of time for grandmothers. They measure a grandchild's growth not in years or months but by how many afghans they've knit them.

"You know my grandson Luke, he's Pearl and Roy's boy, well he's already five afghans along. My land, I don't know where the time goes."

I also noted, with a smile, that the more Iris complained about the work to be done, the more she was very obviously in love with it. All those cookies and squares and comforters were much more than just precious gifts to her family. They were keeping her alive. We should all have such wonderful burdens this time of year.

Library Cops Shake Up a Good, Old Reader

Recently I got another one of those wake-up calls I sometimes get in this Bedford Falls life of mine. I walked into a public library in Regent Park and noticed that they had uniformed library cops—guys stationed right out there in full view with the jacket, striped pants. The whole nine yards. I couldn't tell whether or not they were packing. I didn't see them draw down on anybody "All right, Poindexter! Put your hands in the air and walk away from the thesaurus!"

They more than likely didn't have guns. They're library cops after all. They've probably got rubber stamps in holsters or maybe just big old heavy books that they throw at bad guys. That's not as dumb as it sounds. I'm reading a copy of *War and Peace* right now that could drop an elephant.

Anyway, I guess they're there to make sure nobody starts anything. But what kind of trouble do you start in a library? The worst thing I've ever seen happen in a library is somebody leaving a booger under a desk. Do they have bad characters coming in off the street, selling crack in the children's section?

"There ya go my man. Now you can smoke that in a box, you can smoke that in your sox..."

Are there library hookers? I hadn't even thought of that.

'Hey Bookworm...lonely? Show me your *Harry Potter* and I'll show you *Where the Wilds Things Are*." Ick.

Maybe I'm making too much of it. Maybe these guys just take overdue books really seriously?

We don't have a lot of trouble in the library of my little town. At worst, we have to deal with irate book club members fighting over the last copy of *The Kite Runner* or the odd kid trying to sneak a *National Geographic* into the bathroom.

In fact, in my George Bailey naivete, I had always just assumed that a library to a troublemaker was like salt to a leech. Thugs usually walk across the street to avoid the library, afraid someone might open the door as they passed and a gust of warm, literate air might spread some culture on them.

Library cops. It shocked me mostly because libraries have always been semi-sacred places to me, places where knowledge and quiet rule over ignorance and noise, places where anyone and everyone, regardless of sex, race, religion or status can go and grow and dream—for free. I can't think of another institution that offers that kind of a bargain, although Dairy Queen is a close second.

So when I see a library in need of security, my hackles go up. I feel like something at the very core of my being is under attack. I get the same feeling when I see metal detectors and closed-circuit cameras in public schools. I feel like the good guys are losing.

Why isn't it the other way around, I ask myself. Why aren't the druggies and the thugs and the bullies being forced out of their turf by book-toting, apple-cheeked kids? Why aren't the hookers and pimps and gang-bangers holding noisy, panicked meetings to figure out what to do about all the readers in their neighborhood?

The world is upside down.

CHRISTMAS RITUALS MAKE THE DIFFERENCE

Only a few more sleeps before the big day. This Christmas has got me thinking a bit. Not so much about what to buy or bake—or even what I'm getting—but how to make it special again. Keeping the delight in Christmas is easy when our children are little.

Their belief in the magic and their faith in the wonder of it all are so deeply contagious that you cannot help but have some of it rub off on you. When I watch the videos of those early Christmas's with the kids, it's obvious that Suzanne and I are having at least as much fun —maybe more—as the boys.

But what do you do as the years go by and those chubby-cheeked little imps you had to help get to sleep on Christmas Eve are now lanky lumps with size 11 feet that you have to help get out of bed on Christmas morning?

Where does the magic come from when it's no longer arriving in a sled pulled by eight tiny reindeer? Well, I think it comes from where it always came from, really—inside us. As much fun as it is to watch our kids' faces light up when they open those toys we had such fun picking out, I think that when our children get a little older is when we have the chance to give them the truly special gifts—the things they will treasure forever.

I cannot, for instance, with any accuracy, tell you what Santa brought me for most of the Christmas's of my youth, but I can recount in warm, dreamy detail every little thing about how my mom used to fix us Christmas breakfast.

I can remember exactly how the dining room table was set for our huge extended family Christmas dinners. I can almost taste the little glasses of tomato juice that were at every place setting, every Christmas, even though I never, ever drank mine. I smile and laugh when I see, as clear as if it were yesterday, the dopey, paper Christmas-card hats my grandmother made and which we all wore, year after year.

And of course I cannot ever forget decorating the tree, playing obscene games with the nativity figures and standing uselessly at the foot of the ladder while my father cursed his way through the hanging of the outdoor Christmas lights and electric Santa. Those things and a hundred more like them I have kept in precious memory all these years.

As much as I enjoyed the new hockey sticks and toys, the real gifts of Christmas, the things that keep it magical long after we can no longer hear the patter of hooves on the rooftop, are, ironically, quite commonplace. They are found in the regular, everyday rituals that define us as family. That tell us we are a part of something bigger than ourselves, that remind us of where we come from.

If I never put another present under the tree my kids would be disappointed, I am sure. But if I never put up another tree, never played Nat King Cole's Christmas album from morning to night, never pestered everyone to sit and watch *It's a Wonderful Life,* never made another pot of clam chowder on Christmas Eve again, never did one of the million little, ordinary, everyday, goofy things that make up our Christmas, they would be devastated.

ACTORS SHOULD BE ESSENTIAL EMPLOYEES

I sometimes wonder, usually in one of my unemployed moments, what it must be like to work in an industry where the government has mandated your job security. For instance, people have to have car insurance. You cannot legally operate a vehicle without it. You must file a tax return; something most of us cannot do without engaging the talents of accountancy professionals. It's no guarantee of success, but still, it must be sweet to know that regardless of the economy, Canadian dollar or whatever, people have to buy what you're selling.

Imagine if those same rules applied to actors. In other words, everyone over the age of 16 had to have an actor. Of course you probably wouldn't start off with Orson Welles. Statistics would show, no doubt, that young boys are especially prone to burning out or ruining their actors. The Actors' Bureau would have hundreds of tables proving that men under the age of 21 are much more likely to be involved in a performance accident than, say, young women. They would, therefore, institute a graduated system of actors. Start the kid out with a mime for a year or so and then work him up to an extra before finally allowing him to have full use of a genuine, theatrically-trained thespian. Just getting a kid safely out of his teens would employ a lot of performers.

If all this sounds silly, think for a moment. There are any number of times when an actor would come in very handy. That get-together you'd planned with the new neighbors is tanking horribly. You seem to have nothing in common and conversation is like pulling teeth. Simply dial 1-800-Noel-Coward and within minutes an actor is at your door to make your do the event of the social season. Or perhaps the boss wants you to take the new client out to dinner the same night you normally play poker with the boys. No worries. One phone call, a little makeup, and you can be in two places at once.

Of course, staying with the insurance model, the minute you called your actor for help in an emergency one of two things would necessarily occur. He would either jack his rates up astronomically for the next time you need him or he would cancel your policy, referring to you as a bad entertainment risk.

You would phone your actor and try, in vain, to explain how your surprise birthday party mishap was not your fault—that someone else gave it away. Your actor would ring his hands and explain to you that, in spite of record profits being posted by every actor in Canada, most of that money was being paid out to unscrupulous individuals committing acting fraud—unsavory types, bleeding the acting industry dry by submitting claims for the services of a performer when, in fact, an author or public speaker might have sufficed.

Eventually, your actor would graciously take pity on you and allow you to keep paying him for his services. Your rates would skyrocket of course and you'd have to increase your deductible. Soon you would learn that for small luncheons and book club meetings you'd be better off not calling your actor at all. You'd just learn how to tell a few jokes and juggle.

Yep, that'd be nice.

MAN, DO I EVER LOVE ROAD HOCKEY

One of the few blessings to be found in this pathetically neutered winter we're experiencing is a tremendous upswing in the amount of road hockey around.

Nobody's pond is freezing these days and any kid who isn't into water polo is picking up a stick and a tennis ball and heading out to the nearest flat surface to do what Canadian kids for generations have done when their parents can no longer suffer them to be in the house.

I like road hockey. I think I actually enjoy it more now than I did when I was little. For some reason kids really love to have a parent come and join in. Maybe they're thrilled to have an adult taking an interest in them. Maybe they're not getting enough Dad time. Or maybe they just like being able to fire a tennis ball into a grown-up's crotch with impunity. Whichever it is, I'm always made to feel welcome and I'm hardly ever picked last for teams.

Road hockey is the perfect sport for the armchair athlete. As its name implies, it is usually played on the street. A full-grown man can therefore stand in the middle of the playing surface and, with a long enough stick and a little reaching, touch either curb quite handily. I also tell the kids that because my experience and skill level may prove an unfair advantage, I will not allow myself to cross centre ice. The combination of these two factors means that the game can be played pretty much standing still. It is even possible, I've been told, to put in a decent showing with one hand holding a beer.

Of course one cannot simply jump into a game of road hockey. Any kid will tell you that in order to join the game you have to be someone. These identities are usually declared at the top of one's lungs, on a first-come, first-served basis at the outset of the match.

"I'm Wayne Gretzky."

"I'm Sidney Crosby."

"I'm Mats Sundin."

This is not a trifling matter. Life and death battles have been fought over rights to these monikers. However, as a mature player, I rarely encounter much resistance in these matters. I've joined games as much as an hour late and never heard so much as a peep of protest when I cried out,

"I'm Carl Brewer!" or "I'm Chico Maki!" or even, "I'm Alan Eagleson!"

Finally, there is a particular lexicon one must master to truly be accepted into a road hockey game with kids. After one of my first outings I came back home and proudly announced to my wife that the children liked having me there so much they gave me a nickname. They called me "Goal Suck."

I confess there were some tears when she sat me down and explained that "Goal Suck" was not exactly an honorable appellation. That one took a jug of milk and a bag of cookies to get over. Still, I managed to pull it together enough to join a game the next week where, to my everlasting joy, I played well enough to be high-fived by a seven-year-old.

I went to bed with a smile on my face that night.

THE LITTLE THINGS SIGNIFY TRUE LOVE

A couple of days ago I was out shovelling the town shinny rink. This is not normally a task that I mind doing. It gets me out breathing fresh air, gets my heart pumping and it's good karma. But this particular morning things weren't going so well. There was a good deal more snow than I had counted on. My lower back was humming like an over-wound violin string and there was a wind chill that would've given the Franklin expedition the willies. In short, I was sweaty, cranky and only a soggy mitten away from feeling sorry for myself. But then I looked up and, peering through my frost-encrusted eyelids, I saw my wife walking towards the rink with a snow shovel in her hands.

I couldn't have been more in love with her at that moment than if she had been approaching me naked with a six-pack in one hand and a copy of the *Kama Sutra* in the other.

It occurs to me that the things that really make a marriage work, that really keep you bonded to one another, decade after decade, are not necessarily the grand and lovely gestures of passion and devotion. Candlelit dinners, romantic getaways and lovemaking under a waterfall are all well and good, and certainly have their place, but they are window dressing, the veneer, the wallpaper of a marriage.

The bricks and mortar, the foundation of that edifice are far more mundane—the unasked for cup of coffee, the bath towel warmed in the dryer just before you get out of the shower, the volunteered shovelling help. To my mind those things speak of love in far greater measure than anything you can write a cheque for.

I remember, in the midst of my worst days with cancer, my wife, who is by no means a trained medical professional, girding her loins and administering two hypodermic injections to my hip every day. The needles only pricked me, but they rattled her to the bone.

Morning and night for a solid month she sucked it up, bravely took aim and plunged that thing in, apologizing almost to tears if I should jump or flinch at all. This is real love. This is love with muscle and grit and sinew. When you are on the receiving end of this kind of gesture, and I hope you have been, you are left at a complete loss. Awe, I think, is the best way to describe it. And all you are capable of doing at that point is completely blessing your partner and thanking God for his or her presence in your life. That is love.

My wife and I, like most couples, have had many arguments, some of them very nasty indeed. And the things that inevitably bring us back together after such rifts are not the memories of beach strolls or rose bouquets or haute cuisine. I confess I am at a loss to know what brings my wife back to me, but for myself I have only to picture her in -30 degree wind chill, walking towards me with a shovel in her hand, and I am in love all over again.

Snow Days Bring Back Those Cool Memories

No one loves a snow day more than my wife. She especially loves them when the kids get out playing in the stuff. Today is a snow day and Suzanne is over the moon. And why shouldn't she be? These days most parents can count on one hand the number of instances their children happily spend a whole day outside. When was the last time you had to call your kids in for dinner?

It's one of the great ironies of life that nothing will get sleepy children out of bed and to the breakfast table faster than shouting the words, "You guys can sleep in, it's a snow day," up the stairs. You'd think the governor had called with a full pardon. It did my heart a world of good as well to watch them bolt their hot cereal down and begin to eagerly plan their day in the snow.

When they trotted out the door, legginged, tuqued and mittened, a big part of me wanted to go along too. Were it not for the metric tonne of snot in my sinuses, I think I would have.

They and a cadre of equally bundled pals were headed for the huge drifts on a notorious ridge west of town known by local school kids as Killer Hill. I love that. Every child should have a Killer Hill in their life. I did.

Say the words "Bridlewood Hill" to any kid from my neighborhood and you could instantly fill an afternoon with excited reminiscences of snow forts, ski jumps and death-defying toboggan runs. Even writing those two magical words I find myself grinning stupidly, recalling four of us riding Vic Stone, the fattest kid in school, down the icy front of the hill to try and beat the end of recess bell. Good times.

So the boys trotted out for a day of making forts and memories. Shovels over one shoulder, backpacks filled with survival rations—cookies and hot chocolate—slung on the other. They would come back, many hours later, rosy-cheeked and ravenous. Could a parent wish any more?

My wife, like a lot of women, I imagine, has a cellular loathing of video games and time-stealing computer activity. While I am not quite as Stalin-esque on those issues as she, I do agree they are insidious activities to the extent they seem to addict our children and so rob them of days like these. I guarantee, for instance, that even though today is a snow day and a beautiful one at that, there will still be hundreds of children in and around town who never set foot outside. That is tragic.

And so, yes, my wife is ecstatic today. Today she wins and the computer and video games lose. Today the kids win too. My wife is upstairs now, very happily making several large homemade pizzas to surprise her boys with when they stagger in, covered in snow and sleepily grinning. Her mom motor is absolutely purring with joy. Watching that and seeing the bliss radiating off my children, one cannot help but believe that this is how it should be.

Muzak of the Mind Torments Me So!

From the moment I wake up in the morning I have a song in my head. Please don't misunderstand me. This is not a good thing. Do not confuse this with the storied and delightful song in my heart or bounce in my step or even gleam in my eye.

This is more akin to a load in my pants. This is a completely arbitrary, unchosen and generally unwanted tune that plays like a looped eight-track through my cranium until I can focus enough to turn it the hell off.

It's as though I have some malevolent morning man living inside my noggin. He loves his job and he's always on time.

"From the moment your feet hit the floor! Bringing you all the songs you hate and more!"

And he's a patient little jerk too. He doesn't seem to care when I get up, early or late. He's ready to rock with his stacks of wax, the platters that make you madder, the tunes that drive you loons.

I don't suppose it would be so bad if he changed the playlist now and then. I might not mind having some nice, soft ambient tones greeting me in the morning or maybe the inspiration of Mozart or even the thundering wake-up call of Wagner in the shower.

But Abba? Barry Manilow? The Bee Gees? Is this some Faustian penance for having grown up in the 70s?

As it is I have to summon enormous mental concentration to shut them up. It can be done, I've discovered, but I have to harness the focusing power of Uri Geller to do it. I find that if I think only and completely of what I am doing in the exact present, I cannot hear them.

"OK, I am up. I am putting my feet on the floor. Now I am walking down the hall to the bathroom. I am turning the water on. I am stepping into the sh…'Can you hear the guns, Fernando!'

"Shut up! Just shut the hell up! OK, that's better. Now, I am stepping into the shower. I am feeling the water run over me. This feels nice. I am reaching for the shampoo. I am…'Oh Mandy, well you came and you gave without taking. And I sent you away…'

"Shut up! Shut up! Shut… up!"

The weird thing is that it always stops the minute I turn the water off and step out of the tub. Just dries right up. It's like I have some kind of disco poltergeist who loves hearing himself sing in the shower. I don't get it. I can only guess it has a lot to do with me simply waking up enough to control my thoughts. And I'm sure I'm not the only one who goes through this kind of thing. But why disco?

I'll tell you what I'm really afraid of. I'm terrified that this is only the tip of the iceberg. That I, and possibly thousands of others like me, are the victims of some brainwashing plot that took place 30-odd years ago in high school gyms and dance clubs all over the planet. And that one day soon we'll hear a certain tune in our showers, "Night Fever" or "Stayin' Alive" might be appropriate, and then, like legions of platform-shoed Manchurian candidates, we'll finally complete our ghastly missions.

That's what I'm afraid of.

Lessons on the Road

Life is full of little lessons. The universe, it seems, is constantly scrawling out information, directions and timely tidbits on the chalkboards of our lives. The other day, thanks to a flat tire on the 404, I was tutored quite thoroughly.

For starters, it's amazing how utterly alone you can feel in the midst of thousands upon thousands of other motorists. Sitting there, on the shoulder, in my three-wheeled, metal life jacket, watching haplessly as endless rows of healthy automobiles crawled past, I began to feel like an injured dogie on an Old West cattle drive or perhaps the fatally wounded legionnaire, now only a burden to his comrades, who is left behind with some ammo and a canteen of water, his fate in the hands of the desert.

I was waiting for the rubberneckers, those myopic vultures forever mucking up the flow of traffic by slowing down to gawk at roadside tragedies. In this case however, as the roadside tragedy, I discovered people's behavior to be just the opposite.

Unless you're bleeding or on fire, nobody looks at you. When you're just a stranded dope other motorists seem to go out of their way to avoid eye contact. Eye contact, after all, means connection and connection implies moral responsibility, which translates into helping.

So you get the sideways glance—or the look in your direction but never at you. It's as though everyone who goes by is a highly trained actor and you're the camera. They're experts at looking everywhere but right at you. It wasn't so bad, though. I was warm and I had a CAA membership covering my butt.

It was actually kind of pleasant to watch the sun come up, coral pink and gorgeous over the snowy fields to the east. I thought, of course, about changing the tire myself.

But the flat was on the side of traffic and I didn't feel like ending up a dumb statistic. Worse, as it was the morning crush, it would be just plain embarrassing to get run over by a car doing two km/hr.

With my luck I'd probably get my coat snagged and have to walk beside the guy the 40 klicks to the Bloor exit. Anyway, the CAA said it was their policy to tow vehicles off the highway and change the tire on a side road. So I sat tight.

But when Tow Guy finally arrived, an hour and a half later, (by this time I was writing my wife and wondering if I could drink my own urine) he immediately set about changing the tire. Now people began to gawk. And who wouldn't? I could just imagine the stories they were telling themselves about the idiot-man driving the yellow Beetle who couldn't even change a tire.

But what could I do? Short of wrestling the tire-iron out of Tow Guy's hands, I was shafted. Then, of course, Tow Guy starts making it look easy—real easy, kids' play. Showboat starts getting all fancy, spinning the nuts off and whistling—for the love of Pete.

There's a -30 wind chill and he's whistling. Yeah, he was spinning my nuts off all right, right in front of everybody.

I had half a mind to give him an earful but it was bitterly cold out and the cab of his truck was awfully cozy. Another lesson learned I guess.

LEAVING LAS VEGAS BUT
NOT SOON ENOUGH

They say whatever happens in Vegas, stays in Vegas. Thank goodness it does. If whatever it is that makes that place tick ever left there, it'd be tantamount to an Ebola outbreak.

I visited Lost Wages last week on a business trip. Unfortunately, thanks to some weather issues, my three-day, in-and-out junket ballooned into a week-long spiral through Dante's nine circles of hell.

I know many people love Las Vegas. I have seen them. I have been jostled by them in the thousands along Las Vegas Boulevard, commonly known as "The Strip." I have inhaled their cigarette smoke in restaurants, casinos, elevators and yes, even gyms until, unbeknownst to me, I had developed a pack-a-day habit. I have stood beside them in buffet lines as they shovelled in fried food and biscuit gravy by the bucket load. I know many people love Vegas. I, however, am not one of them.

Like Audrey Hepburn or battlefield photos of the Great War, Las Vegas is something everyone should see at some point in their lives. It puts things in perspective. And I think it clearly divides people into two camps. Vegas is like pumpkin pie in that way—you either love it or you hate it. If you've not been, the best way I can describe it is sort of like Disneyland with hookers.

My first day there I think I said "Wow" a hundred times. At times there is nothing else one can say.

Mammoth, gold-plated hotels, "Wow," a life-sized sphinx, "Wow," semi-naked women swimming in giant fishbowls, "Wow."

Then there are those moments and sights for which there simply are no words—the guy strolling through the casino with a beer in one hand and a cigarette in the other at nine o'clock on a Sunday morning. The rows and rows of utterly sad, completely unmoored souls searching for happiness in the screen of a VDT. The ragged, displaced aboriginals lining every street corner, snapping their hockey-card prostitute promos in your face. At one point my companions and I began to collect these, playing dark games of "Got 'em–Need 'em" over lunch.

To be sure, there were moments of great pleasure to be had as well. In a town like Vegas it is impossible to not find something to enjoy. I savoured a T-bone steak the size of my head one night as I watched the sun set over the mountains and the desert.

Still, I had a dull ache in my chest that started only seconds after the first, hysterical ding-ding-ding of a slot machine reached my ears and never really went away until I saw my wife's face at the arrival gate in Toronto. This is, I began to understand, what a fish must feel like when you pull it out of water for any amount of time.

Vegas prides itself on an anything goes kind of attitude. Within its rhinestone-studded arms you can find anything and everything. And if they don't have it yet, you can bet someone is building it. But on our final morning there, as we sat out by the swimmer-less pool and the fake grass and a palm tree that was inexplicably blaring pop music, I realized what I was most craving was something that Las Vegas could not and would not ever provide me with—silence.

PERFECT DAY TO GET IN BALANCE

As I write these words the vernal—or spring equinox—the only day of the year when we enjoy equal measures of light and dark, is exactly one week away. With the exception of National Chocolate Day (OK, this day may not exist just yet, but I can lobby can't I?) this may be my favorite day of the year. It's a day of perfect balance. The one day of the year when the seasons seem not to be in flux. When, for 24 hours, things appear to be resting in exactly the right spot.

I wonder then, might it not be a good day to get ourselves into balance, to put ourselves in exactly the right spot? Just as we are supposed to change our smoke alarm batteries twice a year when we adjust our clocks for daylight saving time, wouldn't it be a good idea if we had one day a year when we could reset our internal mechanisms.

The equinox seems like an ideal time for just that. A national day of rest and realignment. A day when we stop, take a look at what is out of whack in our lives and try to set things right. I'm eating too much and not exercising enough—have to balance that out. I'm angry more than I'm joyful—need to shift perspective. I work more than I play—there's no equilibrium there. I don't have enough chocolate in my life—that's just wrong.

I think this might be a really good thing.

New Year's Day tries, in vain, to be this day, with its resolutions and promises, but, stuck in the darkest, coldest time of the year it cannot hope to do so. There is not enough light; there is not enough balance.

No wonder so few of us are able to stay the course on those diets and guitar lessons and exercise regimens.

But in the perfect, hopeful light of the equinox, everything seems possible. True, it is not the sunniest day or the warmest day or the longest day. But that's not what we want. Our lives, indeed the universe, need light and dark. We need contrast. How else would we know to love the feel of the sun on our skin unless we had slogged through the black cold of winter? How would we know joy unless we had experienced sorrow? How would we understand love if we'd not known indifference or even hate? How could we delight in *The Sound of Music* unless we'd seen *Ishtar*?

We are beings living in a world of constantly contrasting emotions. It seems to me our journey, our *goal*, is to achieve some kind of balance. In that balance, as I understand it, is peace.

So, isn't it kind of a nice idea to take a few moments, maybe even the whole day on March 21, to be still enough to let our inner scale balance itself. To stop twirling, if even for a short while, to allow the compass of our souls to find its own true north. Just for a day. I know I could use that. I mean, if you can't have chocolate, go for a little inner peace.

Waist Not, Want Not Says Old Fogey

I made the mistake recently of trying to buy a pair of jeans from someone other than Jon, my regular clothes guy. There's a reason, I've realized, why Jon is my regular clothes guy. It's the same reason George is my hardware guy and Franz is my car guy. When I walk into any one of their establishments I'm made to feel welcome, special and most importantly, relatively intelligent.

I was downtown recently and I thought, rather than wait until I was home and go over to Jon's store, it might be more expedient to simply pop into one of those hip, noisy, jean emporiums and pick up some trousers. After all, how hard could it be? Jeans are jeans, right? Looking back, it appears I must have undergone a minor stroke or suffered some form of cranial edema at the time. What was I was thinking?

At 47, I do not consider myself at all old. However, the moment one crosses the threshold of one of these stores, the gum-popping, multi-pierced, naked-bellied staff look at you as though there'd been some kind of bizarre tear in the fabric of time and out you'd stepped from the Middle Ages. There was a gaggle of them gathered saucily around the cash (what does one call a group of narcissistic young women? A pout?) None of them moved to assist me.

I imagined they were huffily drawing straws to see who would have to go help Gramps find the diaper section.

"Are you lost?" They would scream, turning me around and around like some geriatric *Paddle to the Sea,* trying to find where the caregiver had sewn my address label.

But I was left alone. A blessing actually, as it took me a good 10 minutes to realize I was thumbing my way through the women's section. I'm sure that got a rousing "ick" from the gelled heads at the cash.

Eventually I made it to the right gender where I began the impossible task of trying to find clothing that didn't look as though it had been torn off a dead dissident. When did our children decide it would be cool to look like something released from Devil's Island? When I did find a dusty old pile of relatively un-shredded pants, I was confronted with a new problem. One of the gum-snappers, sensing a commission perhaps, had slouched her way over to me and offered to help.

"A 36 waist, please," I said. She looked at me as though I were a circus geek. Apparently people on her planet usually died before ballooning to a 36 waist.

After much-practised harrumphing and sighing, she managed to exhume a pair and I stepped into the change booth, desperately missing Jon and his affable, non-judgmental presence. I really didn't even want to try them on at that point, but I could see her tattooed ankles waiting outside the curtain, no doubt anxious to see what kind of spectacle a 36 waist presented itself as. Great. I would be her moon landing—something she could blog about.

What transpired next happened very quickly. I stepped out of the change booth, turned around and got a "Whoa! Studly!" from Gum-snapper.

Consumed with conflicting embarrassment and the sweats, I immediately strode back inside, changed, handed the pants to the sales girl and walked out of the store. If there'd been a trap door in that little booth leading to Port Perry, I'd have taken it.

Run Neil Run—If You Still Can

At what point in my life did I forget how to run?

I was trying to get somewhere in a hurry the other day and I suddenly found myself doing some spastic, arm-pumping, leg-stomping, spine-jarring rumba across the pavement.

I realized, with not a little dismay, that what I was attempting to do was a thing called running—something I used to do—apparently with great ease. But this looked more like someone getting repeatedly Tasered or something that had just stepped off Dr. Frankenstein's lab table. When did I forget how to run?

Running, you would think, is like whistling or snapping your fingers or swiping chocolate bars. Once you learn how, you never forget. But it isn't.

I've come to realize there are a number of skills and activities that, if not practised on a regular basis, atrophy rapidly to the point of complete amnesia. For instance, have you tried throwing a baseball lately? A couple of weeks ago, back when it was spring, I stepped outside with my sons to fire the old pill around for a while. I was horrified to discover that I couldn't even come close to firing the old pill anywhere. The best I could do was an anemic, overhand swish that looked more like I was swatting away gnats than throwing a hardball. And the pill didn't fire anywhere. Instead of that satisfying thwap of a ball rifled hard into leather, I got a pathetic plop, plop, plop as it landed on the pavement, feet short of its intended target. I was horrified. My kids dropped their gloves and ran screaming. They ran easily and effortlessly. They ran like gazelles—salt in the wounds.

This is one of the reasons I try desperately to get out and snowboard and/or ski at least once a winter. I'm terrified of losing the coordination and balance that I worked so hard to attain, and which, frankly, might prove dangerous if not debilitating to relearn at my age. The same thing applies to bike riding, fly-casting and making love. These are all skills that can come in very handy at unexpected times.

There are a number of activities I have easily and even gladly gotten rusty at. I don't do backflips on the trampoline anymore, I can only belch half the alphabet and my armpit fart is a mere shadow of what it once was. I don't mind. Some things are meant to be let go of. But I never thought I would forget how to run. That one hurt. It was as though I could see an ethereal, younger version of myself flying on ahead of me calling out "Come on! Come on! Race you to the corner!" and I couldn't keep up.

I'm not sure that I will ever return to running, at least not like I did when I was younger. Too many football and rugby games have left their legacy in my tendons, cartilage and vertebrae. But that doesn't mean I have to throw in the towel completely. In fact, I've been thinking of employing a hybrid form of locomotion—skipping. I think this might take off. Skipping is fun, makes you feel good and let's face it, nobody forgets the guy who skips into the audition.

Even the Little Things Need to Be Learned

Teachers might be onto something with the concept of the professional development day. It's a good idea.

I taught high school for a few years and I always thoroughly enjoyed and benefited from my PD day lectures and workshops. It's a pity we all don't take PD days. I believe a truly civilized country would offer PD days to its citizens at least once a month. And I'm not even talking about career enhancement. I just think a lot of us could use one day a month to learn how to be a better human. We could call them Personal Development Days.

Wouldn't it be grand if our government picked up the tab for a monthly lecture on art appreciation, medieval history or small engine repair?

Imagine a federally sanctioned and tax-deductible day off to spend in the museum or gallery of your choice. How nice would that be?

Of course I may be putting the cart slightly ahead of the horse. Perhaps I need to scale my ambitions down a tad. Before we can get folks lined up for a Picasso exhibit or a Hemingway lecture we may need to introduce a few more offerings at the applied level.

Still, there's undoubtedly great merit in a workshop entitled *Stop Driving Like a Jerk, Aim for the Bowl,* or *Understanding the Comb.*

We're all stumbling through this life at our own pace after all, so why not a day set aside to review some basic, but nonetheless useful, skills.

What would be wrong with *Your Dog, Your Crap, How to Get the Cars off Your Front Lawn* or the simple but very important, *Should You*

Procreate? I think we all know folks who might benefit greatly from such offerings.

There are also a whole host of life skills that all of us, for any number of reasons, seem to need constant refreshers on. The following should be nationally mandatory at least once a year:

Listening 101.

The Gentle Art of Thank You.

Apologizing for Dummies.

Beyond Your Navel.

Get the Hell Over It.

You Married Him/Her.

Finally I think we might employ a kind of mentoring system. Each of us, at whichever stage of evolution we're at, has something to offer. The trick would be in establishing a database of sorts that would allow people to pair up in mutually beneficial ways. Bob is a sensitive, intelligent man with a thriving home business that nets him six figures. He has a difficult time, however, meeting women. Ruggedly handsome Carlos doesn't have the brains to pound sand down a rat hole, but he does have a day-planner teeming with steamy assignations. I'm sure the two of them could spend a very profitable day together.

Likewise, Delpheen has a PhD in the classics and can quote Chaucer chapter and verse but she couldn't put a matching outfit together to save her life. Babs thinks a thesaurus was a giant meat-eater, but with a little fabric, a belt and the right shoes she could make Eleanor Roosevelt turn heads. One hand washes the other.

I like the concept of the PD day. We came into this world learning. It would be nice to go out the same way.

Time Travel Easy When You Sit in Sandbox

I was out in the yard this past weekend, raking, cleaning up and like every other living thing around me, feeling reborn in that glorious spring sunshine, when I came across a curious ruin.

Overrun by grass, rotting leaves and fallen twigs, partially hidden underneath the canoe, were wooden timbers framing a square in the earth. I knelt down, brushed away some of the debris and realized with some astonishment that it was, or at least had been, a sandbox.

I knew, of course, that we had a sandbox. I had built it all those years ago. I'd simply been unaware that time was speeding by so quickly. What had once been the focus of the backyard, a hive of truck driving, road paving, city building activity, was now an overgrown, forgotten patch of grass.

I stood there staring at it for a while, feeling myself drifting back in time and then I did something that I knew I shouldn't have done. But I can never stop myself on these occasions. I sat down and began to dig into the past.

Like Gettysburg or Vimy or the Plains of Abraham, anyplace, really, where history has been carved in broad strokes, one doesn't have to go far below the surface of a sandbox before treasures start showing up.

In no time I had a tiny, rusted armada of fire trucks, diggers and assorted toys laid out on the grass beside me. There were undoubtedly more vehicles resting in the strata further down, but I decided further desecration might incur the wrath of the toy gods.

Besides, these few items had more than enough magic to transport me back to a very special time. All stages of child-rearing have their blessings but I think, if pressed, most parents would agree that the sandbox era is a particularly wonderful period for adult and child.

When I wasn't in there with them, I remember clearly sitting not far away, ostensibly reading a book, but unable to tear my gaze away from the earnest little bodies squatting like diapered Brahmins in and around the sand pile. So involved, so completely present were they in their make-believe world that the air above their heads fairly shimmered with thought.

Time stands still for young children when they are at play. I think that's the reason we often have to call them two and three times in for lunch—if they hear us at all. As adults such moments of timelessness—I call them moments with God—are rarer and rarer. I usually get them when I'm writing something I'm completely lost in or when I'm idly paddling my canoe in some particularly beautiful place. When something finally does come along to break the reverie in these moments, one realizes, with shock, that perhaps hours have passed unnoticed. This is sandbox time. Which, I guess, is not really time at all but pure enchantment.

So, could I be blamed for taking a handful of those sandy, three-wheeled talismans out of their tombs and up to the house? I told myself I only wanted a few keepsakes of when the boys were little, but who's kidding whom? I'm hoping that like Aladdin, if I hang onto these long enough or rub them in just the right way, a little of that magic might come my way again.

Goodie Two-shoes Lifestyle on the Verge of Change?

It pains me to admit it but, up until this point in my life, I've been a colossal goodie two-shoes. I have been very well behaved. I have done what I've been told. I've toed the line. No one ever needed to worry about Neil. No sir. He'd be just fine. No smokes hidden in his underwear drawer, no girlie magazine under the mattress, no need to measure the level in the liquor bottles. Everything by the book, on the level, according to Hoyle.

I've never smoked a cigarette, never been intoxicated, never even thrown up on a friend. Somehow I avoided all of that stuff. I'm not sure how that happened. My four brothers and my sister certainly had their share of normal experimental moments growing up and my father, in his teens, could've given Marlon Brando a run for his money. Yet they all grew up, and through those moments, to become reasonably well-adjusted adults.

Three of them became police officers.

I, however, recoiled from danger or misadventure at every turn. Worse, I felt compelled to save those around me from crossing over to the dark side. Once, on a walk with my sister, she swore me to secrecy as she whipped out a Craven A and lit up. She may have interpreted my open-mouthed, ashen-faced visage as tacit agreement but immediately upon returning home, I finked. I ratted her out big time. I sang like a canary. By the time her grounding was up, we'd put a man on the moon. She didn't speak to me for about a year, but that was small penance for saving her immortal soul. Cigarette smoke in her eyes, she'd clearly failed to see the peril she was in. I, however had witnessed the gates of hell opening up to swallow her.

That was my adolescence. Years later, marriage would somewhat temper my monkish zeal. Through the patient, loving instruction of my naughty Quaker wife, I began to understand that things like alcohol, coffee, and gin rummy would not turn me into a wretched combination of Whitney Houston and Robert Downey Jr.

Still, the odd single-malt aside, I remain an inveterate bet-hedger, a dyed-in-the-wool Timid Tammy, a Careful Carl. And that irks. It bothers me because, in my quietest moments, I understand that none of this behavior is based on any grand desire for a better, safer, more ethical or moral existence. It is all based in fear—fear of screwing up, fear of standing out, fear of falling down. Any way you slice it, that's too much fear. And that is no way to live.

Well, enough is enough. On the eve of my 47th birthday I am determined things are going to change. The envelope will be pushed. I have already engaged in behavior I would've deemed unthinkable scant months ago. I have not flipped my mattress in weeks. I am recklessly ignoring "Best Before" dates on dairy products. And I recently made a lane change without indicating. Mind you it was three in the morning on a stretch of deserted country road, but I remind you gentle reader, a journey of a thousand miles begins with a single step.

When It Comes to Running the Show, Mom Rules

This Mother's Day has got me thinking—ticked, actually. I'm wondering who the first male bonehead was that decided we should run the show—that the world needed to move from matriarchy to patriarchy, Goddess to God, Mother Earth to Father in Heaven.

We had a pretty sweet deal there for a very long time. All we had to do was go out and hunt or fish with the boys now and then, throw together a canoe or shelter here and there, maybe fend off the odd desultory raid and the rest of the day was ours. The women did everything else and they did it remarkably well. They cooked, farmed, made our clothing, chose the leaders and raised the children. They made important decisions.

In many native cultures when a man married he lived with his wife's clan. Children belonged to the mother's people. Generally, men hung out around the fire, smoking, swapping stories and comparing loincloths. We got to play with our children. And when we grew tired of that we would see if we couldn't make some more children. Nice work if you can get it. Who was the idiot who thought that needed to be changed?

This Mother's Day, as I stop and look around the world, I don't think the patriarchy thing is working too well. In fact, I think it's a bit of a square peg in a round hole. I may be wrong but I don't think a world ruled by women—or even a world where rule was equally shared by men and women, would've allowed the wholesale slaughter of so many children in so many wars. Nor would it favour one sex over the other, exulting and spoiling its male offspring while keeping its daughters ignorant and servile. I'm just guessing here, but I think the pain of childbirth greatly raises the currency of all children for women.

I'm not slamming men. I like men. Men are very good at a lot of things. We can make a dovetail joint so tight it'll last 100 years, we can run and jump and shoot a puck with breathtaking accuracy. We barbecue a mean steak. We can piggyback children all day long. We can move couches and fridges and armoires. But we are lousy rulers.

Our track record stinks. After violently wresting the stewardship of this planet from our female forbears, what have we done? We have begat a legacy of war, famine, pestilence—and not asking for directions. We have crushed beauty, squandered resources and denied nature at every turn. We've had our destructive little joy ride. It's time to hand back the keys.

The nicest, happiest, most intelligent men I know are those who have a clear and valued feminine side to them. They have balance, strength tempered with sensitivity, aggression with artistry, anima and animus, stripes with solids. Personally, I've had it with sabre-rattling and spear throwing. I'd like to get back to piggybacking those children.

And so, as we recognize Mother's Day this year, let us perhaps do so with an eye to the future and an ear to the past. Let us venerate and respect the feminine in our culture and in ourselves. I'll see you around the campfire.

My Father Myself—It's Not So Bad

I had a terrifying moment the other day when I realized I was turning into my dad. Don't get me wrong. I love my dad immensely. He's a great guy.

I'd love to be half the man he is. But, for all of that, I very clearly remember, as a kid, watching my dad hosing off the sidewalk, painting the garage floor, going to enormous lengths to level what, to my lazy adolescent eye, looked like already very level patio stones, and all the while thinking, "I will never waste a perfectly good weekend doing dumb stuff like that." Yet, last Saturday I found myself, power-washer in hand, cleaning off my front steps.

They weren't even really dirty. It was just something I felt compelled to do. Worse, as I was doing it I wasn't thinking of what fun I was going to have later that day or whether or not I wanted chocolate milk with lunch or even if I was going to go down to the mall later and cruise for chicks.

No, I found myself excitedly pondering a dozen other surfaces I could clean off with this thing. Yikes! All I needed to complete the scene was a pair of Bermuda shorts and some dark knee-high socks.

I suppose I shouldn't really be all that surprised. If I'm being honest there have been other indications—telltale signs that I am indeed becoming my father. For instance I have, for some time, taken to hoisting any number of objects up into the rafters of my garage (because that saves space, you know.)

The ceiling above my vehicles, festooned as it is with roped-off paraphernalia, looks like a Smithsonian space exhibit or perhaps the lair of some rare, garden-furniture-collecting arachnid. But it's handy and more importantly, safe.

A person can walk around in my garage and not trip over a picnic table or canoe or barbecue as he might in another, less responsible individual's garage. I also spray WD-40 on anything threaded—just in case.

I buy tools and extra hardware, not because I need them, but because I may need them. You can never have too many U-bolts, self-tapping screws or dimmer switches.

So far I've managed to avoid buying pegboard and mounting my tools in ascending order of gauge, width or length, but don't think it hasn't crossed my mind. I've also become a compulsive coiler.

That was the big tipoff for me, frankly.

The old man was a sea cadet and you couldn't find a length of rope, hose or extension cord in his domain that wasn't beautifully coiled, tied off and stowed. I don't think he even threw out dental floss without first throwing a half hitch into it to take the kinks out.

I don't know where this has come from, this sudden swell of responsibility, preparedness and organization. I was never like this before.

Only a few years ago I wouldn't have been able to tell you where I kept my Christmas lights, let alone have them neatly coiled, taped and labelled "Christmas Lights."

It must be some anachronistic gene that only kicks in after 45. The same one that drives men to buy label makers and alphabetize their CD collection.

CONCEPT OF TIME BETTER SERVED IN THE HERE AND NOW

I'm not sure what I'd do if I came face to face with whoever invented the concept of time. I don't know whether I'd shake his hand or sock him in the gut. Is the idea of time, the counting and quantifying of life as it passes by, a good thing or a bad thing?

On the one hand it's always a relief to know that Aunt Edna's time of departure from the spare bedroom will only be two more days, but on the other, doesn't knowing exactly how much time I've been on this earth precipitate a mental and physical state to match that age? You're only as old as you think you are is a lovely sentiment, until somebody lays a cake down in front of you with enough candles on it to light Ontario Place. Suddenly you think you're pretty old. How much longer and fruitful might our lifespans be if we never knew how old we were? Seen that way, phrases like "Act your age" and "Grow up" are tantamount to a death sentence.

What did we do before the sundial? Were we happier before the hourglass came along? I wonder. If we'd never started keeping time, no one would ever be maddeningly late or embarrassingly early. People wouldn't be able to wag fingers and say things like "I asked you to be here three hours ago!" They'd have to say "I asked you to be here!" To which you could then answer "I'm here."

There'd be no clocks, no alarms, no over-sleeping. There'd just be going to bed and getting up, whenever. Sort of like your first year of college.

When you think about it, what good is time? When we're having a bad time it tends to drag on forever and when we're enjoying ourselves it flies by. And time is rarely on our side. In fact we willingly become slaves to time. Terminally ill people who are given X amount of time left are frighteningly punctual at making their exits. Without time, patients could never say "How long do I have, doc?" And physicians could never pronounce death sentences. They could only say things like "Dude, you're pretty sick" or "Well, you'll either live or you'll die" or "Yikes." All of which are infinitely better than "You've got six months." Why would we ever let anyone else decide how long we can live?

Without the concept of time, there exists no past and no future. There is only and always now. One cannot have regret for the past or fear of the future if there is only now. And one can run up a sizeable credit card tab in the now as well. On the down side, it's hard to pro-crastinate in the now. People would be constantly after us to get things done now, to deal with them and their discomfiting issues—now. Handy dodges like "Let's put it on the back burner" and "I'll get back to you on that" or "We must get together soon" would no longer exist. And of course, there'd be no telling how long Aunt Edna would be in that spare bedroom. Hmmm. I may not know who invented time, but I think I can guess why.

DISCOVERY OF PELLET GUN
A MAN-SIZED THRILL

I spent the past weekend going through my wife's family farmhouse, getting my mother-in-law ready for a move.

I was in the mud room, up to my elbows in rusting cotter pins and endless spools of bailing twine, when Suzanne called me upstairs.

I sullenly trudged up, expecting yet another in a long line of stained sepia photographs of some ancient moustachioed ancestor, or fierce-eyed gaggle of crinolined imperious matriarchs.

However, when I sulked into the tiny bedroom she'd been beckoning me from, my spirits rose considerably. Following her gaze, I peered into the dark recesses of a long-forgotten closet and with the excitement of a tomb raider, I spied the treasure my wife had just discovered.

A pellet gun. Lewis and Clark could not have been more overjoyed at glimpsing the Pacific than I was at the sight of that gleaming wooden stock, that patiently confident barrel, that insouciant trigger.

My initial reaction was to grab it and go giddily dancing outside to show the kids. But after 20 years of marriage I have learned that there are times for giddy dancing and times for fake, spouse-satisfying responsibility. I put on as concerned a face as possible and, cradling the beautiful thing in my arms, muttered something like "…guess I better hide this in the car…safety issues…blah, blah, blah."

My wife, of course, was not fooled for a second. She is a patient, wise woman and has been married to an eight-year-old long enough to know how to handle these situations. She also knows that unlike herself, my childhood and adolescence were conspicuously and torturously gun free. Suzanne, whose name still strikes fear into groundhog communities in the hills of the Hockley Valley, very kindly smiled and let me skip down the stairs with my new toy. She didn't even comment on my high pitched shriek and "Yippee."

I have never had a gun. At least not a real gun that could actually shoot and kill something. In fact, I have always considered myself something of a peace-nik.

Up until this point in our family life we have barely allowed replica weapons in the house. But life is nothing if not dynamic. Times and people change. And while I would never have considered bringing such a thing home when my boys were younger, they are older now and for some reason the discovery of this gun seemed not only timely, but fortuitous. This, I reasoned (or rationalized, choose your poison) would be, at a time when my children are growing up and away from me, a reason to bond once more.

And so I must say I was rather feeling my fatherly oats when I led the lads out into the backyard yesterday for a little target shooting. They were looking at me again with those adoring eyes. Eyes I hadn't seen since building the tree fort or wheeling out a brand new bike or bringing home a puppy.

It felt good. Right up to the point when my wife walked out into the backyard, still wearing her apron, picked up the rifle and potted a bull's eye from 30 yards.

Instantly I felt two sets of adoring eyes coldly shift from one parent to another. Darn gun.

CAMP EXPERIENCE WORTH EVERY PENNY AND MORE

My youngest just got home from almost two weeks of camp. I've never seen a kid so completely, wonderfully happy—happy to be home and overjoyed with his experiences away. I don't know if you've ever been near someone who is that totally content. There's a force field around them. It's like standing too close to a nuclear reactor—or Tony Robbins. It rubs off.

I never did the camp thing. I went to an athletic leadership camp for a couple of weeks in Grade 11 but it was more like a gulag with wrestling mats. I didn't enjoy my time there so much as survived it. None of my siblings went to any kind of camp that I can recall. There were six of us and the old man would've had to knock over a bank to pay for that kind of thing.

As it was, I'm pretty sure he must've been a heroin mule or a numbers runner on the side, just to keep all of us in shoes. Still, I don't think any of us ever felt like we missed out on the experience. With six kids in the house, five of them boys, our place was really a lot like camp. We had bunk beds, hazing rituals and we generally had to line up for the shower.

But camps have also changed a great deal since I was a kid.

We never had arts camps or computer camps or quantum physics camps like they have nowadays.

Our options were shambling, run-down old places with names that sounded vaguely scatological—Camp Tay-ka-Poo and Camp Whiz-a-Way. Places with leaky roofs and torn screens, where some one-eyed, crusty old badger named Buck would teach you to swim by throwing you off the dock and at least once a summer there was a fatality on the archery range. That was camp.

My son's experience was, thankfully, a great deal different than that. He spent 10 days at DIAC, (Durham Integrated Arts Camp) where he had the time of his life. He's a different kind of kid in that while he enjoys canoeing and biking and stuff like that, he's also working his way through most of Kurt Vonnegut's novels and can hold his own in a discussion of existential determinism. And while you love a kid like that to death, you also worry about him sometimes. You worry that his gifts, those things that make him priceless in your heart, might make him an outsider in the eyes of the heartless.

And so it was that my worries and fears were completely and joyfully allayed when, on Parents' Day (and trust me you never really feel more like a parent than when you visit your kid at a camp on Parents' Day) he quietly and happily confided to me that he never knew there were so many other kids like him around.

In that moment I could literally see him shedding the burdensome yoke of different and donning the mantle of pride. They could've charged me a million dollars for my child to experience that moment and I would gladly have paid it.

Never Underestimate a Simple Gesture

I must have done something horribly wrong in another life, something unspeakably vile. Otherwise, why do I find myself standing in front of my house at three in the morning in my boxer shorts, staring helplessly up at a neighbor's window where a dog seems to be imprisoned?

Actually, it sounds more like a dog has been impaled or perhaps disemboweled and set on fire, such is the din, the absolutely spine-shattering wailing coming from that window. Typical of these scenarios, of course, only my wife and I seem to be able to hear this. The occupants of the house (the dog's captors) seem blissfully unaware of its sufferings. Remarkable. And now there is a wild, panicked scratching to accompany the mad howling, as though the poor beast were attempting to claw through the masonry to escape its torment.

However this ends, someone is in for a fair chunk of drywall work and quite possibly a hefty plumbing bill. Hapless and helpless, I go back to bed where my wife and I close the windows and put pillows over our heads.

The next day we are visited by a friend. After a phone conversation in which my wife had mentioned, in passing, that she was feeling tired and a little stressed, this kind soul had decided to pay us a visit. She arrived, unannounced, with a bottle of wine, some cheese and a smile simply because she wanted to make someone feel better.

As they say on English exams, compare and contrast these two situations. On the one hand we have irritation, pain and suffering in animal and human as the result of an uncaring, selfish perspective. On the other, we have peace, harmony and happiness as the result of one simple act of kindness and consideration.

It has come to my attention, after some 47 years of experimentation and observation, that the route to this planet's salvation lies not in science or chemistry or invention of any kind, but in simple courtesy. Nothing, in my estimation, has greater transformative power for good than the elemental act of thinking of others, of being aware of the fact that we do not live alone—that everything we do or do not do will impact someone for better or worse. The cumulative effect of choosing to act for the better is incalculable. All of us can point to at least one instance in our lives where some loving individual's unbidden kind word, phone call or gesture made us feel instantly better and our lives easier and more comfortable.

What we may have more trouble remembering though, are those moments when our own selfish thoughtlessness has had the opposite effect on those around us. Moments that could've easily been avoided had we only paused to think. Does everyone in the neighborhood really want to hear my music? How many trucks on the front lawn is too many? Is my dog keeping anyone up? Never underestimate the scope of such seemingly innocuous decisions. The world turns easily or not on such choices.

All of us have enormous power to change lives on a daily basis. The domino effect that I begin by letting in or cutting off that other driver in the morning, by smiling or frowning in the office elevator, by complimenting or nitpicking my child or spouse, is like the storied hurricane begun by the flapping of a butterfly's wings. Think and choose wisely.

MORE MATRIMONIAL EFFORT COULD HELP AVOID DIVORCE CRAWL

Recently there was a newspaper story about a woman who planned to crawl, in her wedding dress, for eight hours to mark her failed marriage. Dressed in white, veil and all, hands and knees, to eight different stations around the city, commemorating her eight years of wedded hiss. Sort of a "Via Divorce-osa."

Why, one might ask? Well, aside from the obvious laughs inherent in such a venture, apparently she needs to rid herself of the emotional baggage in order to be truly ready for a new relationship. This, by the way, from a marriage that purportedly ended very amicably. No abuse, no maltreatment, no alcoholic rage. Some people can find baggage anywhere I suppose. Some people love baggage. All I can say is, good luck to the next guy she meets. In fairness, I should point out that this woman is also a performance artist. I love that title. I love performance artists. These are the people who rent Massey Hall so they can protest the plight of the nearly extinct African horned puss worm by taking a bowel movement on stage in front of 10,000 paying customers. Wow, the medium is the message, I suppose.

One can only ponder how much fun marriage to people like this must be.

"Honey can you take the kids to soccer practice?"

"Of course I can't take the kids to soccer practice! I'm creating."

"I thought you were creating all morning."

"Oh you plebe…that wasn't creating, that was pondering."

"Oh."

"You're standing in my aura!"

"Sorry."

Because I'm a man, I also can't help but wonder what the male equivalent of this divorce crawl might be? Probably a brisk stroll to the nearest wing joint, followed, several hours later, by a crawl home.

We've all met people like this crawling woman. Most of them haven't gotten to the point where they actually label themselves performance artists, but that is essentially what they are. For people like this, it's all about the drama. They drink pain and breathe upset. They're never truly happy until they're wretched. And even that wouldn't be so bad, I guess, if they didn't feel constantly compelled to share their misery with the rest of us.

Isn't there enough drama in the world—*real* drama—without having to cook some up where none really exists? The crawling lady apparently has been training for this jaunt for more than six months, the last month and a half spent actually crawling, in gymnasiums, parks and on the street. Her ex, too, has been involved, generously creating a re-mix of their wedding song as a sound track for the film of this silliness.

I can't imagine how much energy it will take this woman to crawl for eight hours around the streets of Toronto on a hot, August day. Not to mention the amount of energy and focus put into planning, publicizing, filming and mounting a website for the whole fiasco. What is interesting to consider however, is what that amount of energy, imagination, creativity and passion might have done to keep her marriage together eight years ago. But there's not much drama in a marriage that works, is there? And who wants to watch that?

I don't much care for flying anymore. The novelty wore off somewhere between 9/11 and my last cavity search. I don't even care if I get a window seat anymore. I prefer the aisle. Looking out the window only reminds me of how far we have to plummet should the law of gravity suddenly kick in. On the aisle I can at least stretch one of my legs out, bringing a measure of relief to feet that, above 10,000-feet elevation, now swell to the size of rugby balls.

I used to fly without a care in the world. The aircraft could be in the middle of the worst meteorological pounding imaginable, drinks, magazines, briefcases and cabin stewards ricocheting madly off the fuselage walls and I'd be oblivious. Now there are at least two moments per flight, usually takeoff and landing, when I am viscerally aware of the potential for disaster surrounding me. At these moments I always run the same scenario through my head; I send a silent prayer to my wife, children and agent (an actor is always an actor) and then I find myself looking about me and wondering, in the event of a crash, how on earth am I am going to lead these people to safety.

Flying is a wonderfully accurate litmus test of manners, too. Upon landing, I always watch to see who will be the first moron to stand up and reach for his luggage while the plane is still taxiing to the gate. I'm always delighted when the plane hiccups at these moments, sending the idiot whose schedule is so much more important than the rest of ours careening into a bulkhead. Poetic justice.

I am also enormously entertained and ultimately vexed by what passes for carry-on luggage with some people. I have seen individuals attempting to cram what amount to steamer trunks into the overhead bins. These people think nothing of holding up the entire plane while they and their Sherpas take up every square inch of storage space within a 10-foot radius of their designated seat.

I'm weary of all the flying games as well. I don't find nearly the enjoyment I used to in "Share the arm rest," or "Recline in my face," or even "Worst Aim—the bathroom game." And all of these irritations are nothing compared to the indignities one endures at the security gate. I have seen S & M enthusiasts tire of such abuse.

Thankfully, for the airline industry and the human race in general, there still exist those rare virtues of kindness, patience and selflessness. Last week I sat across the aisle from a young couple and their infant daughter. The child had a head cold and on our descent into Toronto her ears and sinuses caused her to scream in pain.

She wailed until I could feel the daggered eyes of the entire cabin burning towards the three of them. Still she sobbed and thrashed. She cried so hard she vomited. Now the steely glares were hurled like spears. I felt terribly for them. Anyone who has travelled with children would.

I was searching for something to say or do when the stranger sitting behind them put his hand on the father's shoulder, caught his frantic eye and simply smiled. In that moment of connection, in the relief of the father and the compassion of the stranger, I saw what keeps the world and the airlines in business.

I narrowly escaped some seriously bad karma the other day. I could smell the stink of it as it brushed by me.

An airport limousine was to pick me up for my fourth trek to Regina in a week (the Regina Chamber of Commerce is considering erecting a plaque at the airport in my name). My driver, however, arrived an hour and a half late. Not 10 minutes, not 20 minutes, not even a half hour late—an hour and a half late. That's a quarter-century late in airline time.

By the time he finally showed up, I was more than a little irked and seriously doubting that I could make my flight. But when the poor guy stumbled out of the car I found I just couldn't get angry. He had bed-head that could've given Amy Winehouse a run for her money and the saddest eyes I've ever seen outside an animal shelter.

He was not having a good day. Besides, I didn't want to get angry. I'd been fighting the "angrys" all morning. You know how it goes; you get up, looking forward to a nice day and then, maybe, you stub your toe, or you spill coffee on your shirt—or your driver is 90 minutes tardy. If you let yourself get sucked into that swirling, negative cesspool, the next thing you know your whole day is seriously in the dumper.

I'd fume at my driver, put myself in a nice little mood, then I'd dump all over the airline check-in person, who in turn would have her day ruined and grumpily pass the black cloud along to the next person she dealt with. And so on and so on until somebody finally walks into a post office with an AK-47. It's a hideously perfect chain reaction.

I didn't want that to happen. So, ignoring the ravings of the anal, schedule-worshipping idiot in the back of my head, I smiled at the guy. I told him, "No sweat, if he hustled, really hustled, there was still an outside chance we could make that flight." We could turn this day around.

Somehow, though, I don't think he was completely on board my little ship of hope. Although he began driving like Rob Ford on his way to a pig roast, his hangdog expression and glazed eyes told me he was still nowhere near accentuating the positive. And, sure as shooting, just as I thought we might make it on time after all, with a lurch and a heart-sickening sputter, the limo died.

I sat in the back, laughing uncontrollably, convinced there was a camera somewhere feeding all of this to the Internet or some reality show. My driver however, looked like Barrabas in a suit—a condemned man.

It occurred to me then that although we were both stuck in the middle of the same rotten situation, we were making vastly different choices regarding it. My ship of hope, having struck another karmic iceberg, was sinking, true, but I was the only one now laughing into the lifeboat.

Like a good captain, he'd decided to go down with his limo. I jumped in a cab and left him. My day went on to be quite lovely—the way I'd envisioned it. I wasn't there to see how his played out, but I can guarantee you one thing—good or bad, it was still his choice.

What Did You Do With the Cow?

Years ago, a friend of mine who was doing very well financially, blurted excitedly that he had engaged the services of a clothier.

I wasn't doing nearly so well financially, and wasn't even sure what a clothier was. I thought it might be something vaguely sexual and so dropped the conversation immediately. I have since been fortunate enough to go through the clothier experience just three times; once before my wedding, once when I was handed an obscene amount of money to buy my own wardrobe for a TV show, and once, in the last year when I simply lost my mind.

In a nutshell, a clothier is someone who knows you are a sartorially challenged idiot with no sense of style and, for a fee that rivals the GNP of a small South American country, happily avails you of his.

Walking into a clothier is like stepping into a high-priced fabric brothel. Soft, manicured hands swiftly guide you to a place of satin pillows and leather chairs. Cigars and coffee are proffered, fingers are snapped, hands are clapped and, one by one, bolts of rare cloth and all manner of breath-taking garments are paraded past for your enjoyment.

Succulent figs are popped into your mouth. An Armani-clad eunuch silently refills your cappuccino, then slinks out of sight behind a rack of blazers.

These men are like magicians—dark magicians who smell really good. No words need be spoken, no choices made. They know exactly what you want, even if you don't. Using an intoxicating blend of flattery, fawning and exquisitely timed chuckling they weave a spell so thoroughly and enjoyably narcotic that soon enough, you, like they, see nothing at all askance in a pair of $150 gotchies.

Eyes glazed, you can only smile and nod as a crack team of tailors move, ninja-like, around your body. Chalk dust flies like cocaine at a Hollywood housewarming, tape measures cut through the air with the grace of a maestro's baton and in less time than it takes to turn your head and cough; an inseam is discreetly measured.

More cappuccino, more figs, more laughter. Everything you say today is pure genius. You're the wittiest man alive, and at approximately $50 bucks a laugh, you ought to be.

Next, come shirts and ties. Secret drawers and panels are opened revealing the private stock—the stuff they don't show to just any old fool. No, no, my friend, only an imbecile with your discerning tastes can appreciate a tie that costs more than your last car payment.

Suddenly, a ghastly faux pas. A bumbling novice's error has left a price tag briefly but carelessly in view. You shudder as a momentary spasm of sanity darkens the skies of your present nirvana. Luckily you're dealing with professionals. In a flash they recognize your hesitancy and are on it like a button-down collar.

Out of nowhere, yes-men, professional sycophants appear and skillfully administer the "Hind-lick" maneuver until your pulse returns to normal. There is one final moment of embarrassment as you lock up in spastic terror while signing for it all, but once again, gentle manicured hands help you press pen to paper.

When you come to, you are standing in your kitchen holding a garment bag and looking very much like Jack holding a sack of worthless beans and your wife wants to know what you did with the cow.

Teen Terrors

In the next 14 days my sons will turn 13 and 16 years of age, an event so cataclysmically overwhelming it rivals a complete solar eclipse, ice age or perhaps a Leaf Stanley Cup victory.

I am unquestionably not the first parent to go through this, but that doesn't lessen the impact any. And I am discovering that those who have gone through it, like airplane crash survivors or Vietnam veterans, are loathe to talk about their experiences. The mere mention of those years is accompanied by facial ticks and glassy-eyed thousand-yard stares. This is something, apparently, one must face on one's own.

For the first time in our lives, my wife and I will have two teenagers on the premises. And don't misunderstand me, it's not the number that is the issue. In the past we've had many teens in the house at various times, but as we had no biological bond with most of them we happily and eagerly kicked them out when the hormonal funk level went off the charts. We can't do that with these two. We made them.

After experiencing our first teenager's behaviour, I had voiced, I thought reasonably, that one more would simply amount to twice the laundry, sarcasm and rolling of angst-ridden eyes.

But friends and relatives who have been there and lived to tell the tale, have made it plain that, while this is true, there is exponentially more to contend with when a second—or worse yet, a third or fourth is added to the mix.

Teenagers, apparently, are like Siamese fighting fish. One is fine. He swims comfortably, if moodily around his bowl and minds his own navel-gazing business. But the moment you place another of his kind within sight, he becomes truculent, territorial and completely unreasonable. By the by, females—again, I am told—are far and away the worst. This is why you don't see any female Siamese fighting fish. They killed each other off years ago over a prom dress issue.

Still, the gasoline on the fire here, the real ghost in the machine, is the 16 thing. Sixteen, as I recall, is that mysterious demarcation line where gangly, moody boys suddenly become either gunslingers or poets—strident, authority-challenging Turks or emotionally mired artistes with hair-trigger world-weariness and calloused diary fingers.

In my own case I was something of an anomaly, a poem-slinger for lack of a better phrase. I would happily knock people down on the football field for hours then closet myself with journal and pen, a sort of Franz Kafka in gym socks.

When this happens you may as well have a foreign exchange student living under your roof. No one seems to understand them. And although they and their siblings may only be separated by a scant year or two, in the eyes of the older the younger may as well be wearing diapers. Enter Siamese fighting fish.

Thus far my children get along quite well. There is the occasional dust-up that generally doesn't last long and it's usually nothing that a half-hour in headphones and music can't cool out. And they seem to like us too.

Still, I know that in two weeks time, on the eve of the 12-year-old's 13th birthday, I'll be as anxious as I was on Dec. 31, 1999, wondering if, when I awake the next day, the peaceful world as I know it will be gone forever.

She Knows How to Fix It

I'm sure my friends and family have been aware of this for years, but I am finally beginning to realize that I'm not great in a crisis. You know in the movies, when the plane is going down, there's that guy with the lantern jaw and the chiselled good looks who stands up and says in a perfect baritone, "Don't worry folks, this baby isn't going down on my watch."

Well, I'm not him. I'm not even the guy beside him. I'm the guy in the back of the plane tearing at his seat belt, screaming, "We're all gonna die! We're all gonna die!"

This is not to say I am incapable of rising to a challenge. I can and almost always do eventually remedy the current disaster. But not before I've first assured myself and everyone within earshot that this time we're totally screwed. My initial reaction to even the most mundane household emergencies, for instance, is reliably way over the top.

"The knob is loose on the cutlery drawer! Oh, that's it, we're moving!"

You can imagine the stratospheric heights of panic I can reach when something more substantial transpires. News of an electrical job will find me in the fetal position moaning incoherently about amperages and current. Any carpentry involving more than Grade 2 math leaves me chewing antacids like they were Halloween candy.

And the mere whiff of a water issue, be it a leaky roof, burst pipe or my arch-nemesis, Lord Sump Pump, and the eyes roll back in the head and I begin to flop around on the ground like a newly landed trout. It's not pretty.

Fortunately I have a wife who is a doer. We are perfectly matched in that, when disaster strikes, the back of her hand is an exact fit for my screaming mouth. My wife is completely fearless in these matters. In fact, I secretly believe she enjoys them. There is a remarkably attractive part of her that only really comes alive in moments of great trial.

Some men buy their wives skimpy negligees or provocative evening wear to get their male motors running. Not me. I go to the hardware store. I've never seen my wife look sexier than when she's holding a blowtorch or a chainsaw. Weird? Maybe, but it's how we make it work. My wife is also, bless her crowbar wielding heart, very sensitive to my hair-trigger male ego.

She has become, over our 22 years together remarkably adept at stroking and pushing at the same time. Through this wonderful combination of what, for lack of a better phrase, I'll call supportive badgering, I have gone, on occasions too numerous to mention, from catatonia to handyman. It's not a short journey and it's not one I like much—but it's always good for me.

It's sort of like a do-it-yourselfer intervention. Only there's only ever two chairs at the meeting—hers and mine. But each time I get a little less shrill, a little less like the last chick alive in the horror movie and a little more like a man.

If you can find somebody who does that for you, buy her a blowtorch.

Being in Contact With Someone Not the Same as Being in Touch

I receive and often send sometimes dozens of emails each day. Most of these are very brief, to-the-point replies or requests for information of some sort. I rarely talk on the phone anymore and frankly, I can't remember the last time I wrote a letter by hand. Thanks to the Internet and the world of instantaneous communication that we live in, I'm probably in contact with more people than ever, but hardly in touch with anyone.

As much as I love this high-tech age, (and believe me, when I can have all three of the original *Charlie's Angels* on my desktop for free, why wouldn't I love it?) I'm realizing there is a price to be paid for all of this speed and efficiency. It seems to me, that as we've become experts at shorthand texting and zipping vowel-less, truncated barbs back and forth that are guaranteed to make us LOL, we are talking more and saying less. We are losing the ability to really connect with one another in meaningful ways.

This past weekend I took part in two very important celebrations; my father's 80th birthday and my son's 13th. We had a very nice, very fun party for each. People had a good time. And yet, I could not help but feel that in both cases something was lacking, the same thing, actually—connection.

I love my father so much it hurts sometimes. And although he is still hale and quite hearty at 80, I am viscerally aware of the temporality of his presence in my life, of both he and my mother who is equally dear to me. Likewise is my 13-year-old a gift from God to me. Both my boys are. I sometimes look back and wonder what the hell I called that monochromatic, placid existence I lived before I had children. These people are hugely important parts of me.

Yet, did I mention that fact to either of them this past weekend? Did I, or anyone else, stop the music, shut off the Leaf game, or the video games long enough to clear my throat, look into their eyes, smile and tell them something as simple as "You have made my life immeasurably better simply by your presence in it?" No. I, we, did not.

I do not mean to say that those sentiments, those emotions were not present in the hearts of everyone there, on both occasions. I know they were, in spades. But we have all become so rusty at doing what used to be very easy for us; sincerely communicating our feelings, that we now prefer to keep the volume up, the cake lit and the presents coming. We must keep moving, because if we stop long enough, our throats will begin to close and our eyes to well up because our hearts have something they desperately want to say.

I long for the days of heartfelt speeches, sappy toasts and weepy tributes and, having taken myself to task on this issue, I am henceforth committed to keeping ritual and meaningful communication in my celebrations. I would like to think that many years from now—when my father, mother or any one of the dozens of people who are precious to me in this life, finally passes—that the loss may not be so numbingly devastating as I will have already told them on countless occasions how much I love them.

CONNECT WITH A VET THIS REMEMBRANCE DAY

November. Grey, damp mornings, harsh winds carrying the promise of winter's chill, barren, brown, frosted landscapes. The season of Remembrance. Some people have a hard time with November. The days are short, the nights are long and cold and wet, everywhere everything seems to be withering and in the distance one can just make out the blaring, gaudy roller coaster of December approaching. It can be a bit of a downer.

Personally though, I like the month. I find it a very introspective time of year, a perfect month for walks and thinking and reflection, an apt milieu to the Armistice and our Day of Remembering.

I hope this year that you and your family will be able to find meaning in this day. It's not hard. One has only to spend a short time in the company of those shambling, shuffling old men and women in the blue blazers and berets. Even a shared minute of silence with them is enough to effect change in a heart hardened by the hustle, bustle and blaring inanity of day-to-day life.

And if you want to really understand what Remembrance Day is all about, do what I do. During that moment of silence do not bow your head. Do not close your eyes and think about how much time is left or how cold it is or about the next item on your day's itinerary. Instead, look at the eyes of the veterans. Many of them do not bow their heads. Indeed, I have found that most of them are looking up at something far, far away and yet intensely close to them. In those moist, cataract-clouded eyes you will see untold pain, heartache, horror, courage, pride and love—an enormous amount of love. You will see flashes of a frightened, confused, excited young man or woman. You will see things that, thanks to that vet, you and I have never had to see.

I warn you however, it's not easy. There is always a price to be paid for connecting to another human being.

When you stare into those eyes you open a conduit that flows both ways. And when you allow their sacrifice to pass into your own heart, this grey day in November will never be the same for you again.

Finally, you may experience, as I often do, the intense desire to hug one of these people or to at least shake one of their hands and offer a heartfelt "Thank you."

But please, don't make the mistake, as I have done in the past, of ignoring this impulse. Do it. Do it on Remembrance Day. Do it on the days before and following November 11.

If you find yourself in the company of a vet or the mother or father of a vet or anyone who has made any kind of sacrifice for our freedom in the past or the present, let them know with a hug, a handshake, a smile or salute, that you are grateful. And most importantly that you will never, ever forget.

Nothing like a good snowstorm to bring out the guys—at least in a small town. You know who the guys are. They're the fellas gleefully plodding behind the snowblowers, coming to the rescue on riding mowers and at the wheels of snow-bladed pickups. The guys who wait anxiously, pull-cords in hand, for disaster. The guys who live for a good dump…of snow.

You can spot a guy a mile away, even when it isn't snowing. They're usually clad in any combination of duck-canvas coveralls, Kenora dinner-jacket, wool toque and/or baseball cap, fluorescent orange work gloves and, if it isn't snowing or the wind hasn't dropped a tree on someone's car or house nearby, they'll be either tinkering with some form of combustion engine in their driveway or at the Co-op buying more warm stuff to wear—just in case.

If you're lucky enough to live beside or near a guy, you'll never have to shovel an ounce of snow again. In fact, for the paltry fee of a case of beer or a 40-pounder of rye you can usually get four-season coverage out of your neighborhood guy.

He'll happily chainsaw your wood, leaf-blow your yard and power-wash your car, house or children. If it requires a motor and a gas/oil mix, your guy's your man. Mind you, there are limitations. Don't expect your guy to just jump in, plow you out of your driveway and be on his way. No—guys like to talk. Watching a guy work his magic with his blade and then hopping in your car and taking off to work without a word of chit-chat is tantamount to slapping a cow in India or dissing

Merle Haggard at a Lion's barbecue. It's just not done. Not unless you want to find yourself arse-deep in the white stuff next December.

Guy etiquette requires that, when the job is done, you put everything else on hold, tilt your hat back on your forehead, maybe put a foot up on the running board and shoot the breeze for a bit. For those who don't speak Guy here are a few good starters:

"Boy she's sure coming down, huh?"

"Helluva nice rig you got here."

"Anything to get away from the wife for a few hours, eh?"

Avoid comments like:

"Could you keep it off the garden next time?"

"Helluva nice wife you've got there."

"Would you like to come inside for a chai and biscotti?"

Remuneration is a tricky subject. Remember, guys are very much heroes—sort of Robin Hoods in Sorels and they need to be treated as such. Nobody ever turned to Audie Murphy or Errol Flynn after they'd saved the day and said, "Um, can I write you a cheque?"

It's the height of bad form to bring up compensation in front of a guy. It should simply be understood that sometime, in the not too distant future, a little something in the form of a bottle, a case or anything in a casserole dish will make its way to the guy's house. It's an ancient and time-honoured system.

As I say, the recent storm, with its attendant stuck vehicles, blocked driveways and general meteorological panic was like a salt lick for guys. They were everywhere. By midday the air was humming with the sound of two-stroke engines and the only vehicles on the road were manned by happily grinning, hoar-rimed saviours. Bless them all.

Cherish Every Moment You Get to Spend on This Earth

One of the weird habits I've picked up since going through my dance with cancer has been that every Saturday morning, along with my coffee and the pleasant, chatty company of my wife and kids, I spend a few moments glancing through the obituary section of the paper. I don't know precisely when or even why I started doing this but at some point over the last three years it has become a routine—and a surprisingly pleasant one at that.

Far from creepy or morose, the feeling that I get as I look at the faces, young and old, of the recently deceased is remarkably warm and fuzzy. It is as though each one of them, along with the often heartbreaking messages from the families they've left behind, is reminding me in the most profound way of the importance of each day, each hour, each second we draw breath.

Staring down the barrel of my own demise several years ago was infinitely life altering. I am forever grateful for the life lessons my ugly little friend, cancer, taught me. However, like all human beings I tend to be forgetful. Three years clear of a cancer diagnosis, I find myself falling into some troubling old patterns. Worry, fear, boredom and a dozen other equally vile little germs have been cropping up as regularly as in the good old days. Days when I thought I would live forever, when I took my time here for granted.

The obits can be a neat little inoculation against such viruses. Each grainy, black and white photograph, each life boiled down to a paragraph and the stark finality of each birth and death date cut very cleanly to the heart of the matter. We are here for a very short time indeed. Let us not waste a second of it.

Instead, let us stop and look around us, eyes wide, at the blessings and love and joy that are ours for the taking. Let us be still occasionally and listen to the voices of the dead pleading with us to savour it all—the good, the bad, the easy, the hard, the cold and the warm. Life.

One of my favourite sayings came from legendary rocker Warren Zevon who, only months before his death from mesothelioma, the same cancer that killed Steve McQueen, told David Letterman and millions of viewers to "Enjoy every sandwich."

Amen.

So simple but right on the money.

I hope you'll do yourself a favour this year and forget about losing weight or getting fit or writing that novel. Instead, do two simple things that I guarantee will change your life in a million, wonderful ways.

Spend a few minutes listening in the obituary section every Saturday morning and tape the words "Enjoy every sandwich" up on every mirror in your house. If you can make yourself slow down, even a little, you'll give all the great things in your life the chance to catch up with you.

Soon you'll be awash in them. I wish you all the blessings in the world. Happy New Year.

Bird Nerds Have Found a Special Place in my Heart

Keep it under your hat, but I've become a bit of a birder. I don't mean the kind of guy who wears a lot of camouflage gear and squats in the cedars for hours, notebook and field glasses in hand.

I like to think of myself more as a virile, sexy birder—the kind of birder who works out and has to beat off bird-loving chicks with a stick. A Scotch-swilling, bare-knuckle kind of birder. Sort of a cross between Ernest Hemingway and John James Audobon. In any event, I do find these little creatures endlessly fascinating.

We've always had bird feeders of one sort or another around the place. And birds have always been present. I've just never seemed to take much notice of them, nor they me. But this winter my wife started spreading a particular seed on our kitchen windowsill and it's turned that window into a kind of avian aquarium. We can stand quietly at the kitchen sink and they will happily flit in, chow down, keeping a curious eye on the monstrous things with no feathers on the other side of the glass, then flutter off again. In a minute or so they're back once more, snarfing millet and looking at me with what appears to be thinly veiled sympathy; poor dude can't fly and that's a poor excuse for a beak.

I find myself spending enormous amounts of time at that window, grinning like an idiot. It may just be the storyteller in me wanting to anthropomorphize everything in sight, but they really do seem to have personalities. Some are much braver—or perhaps just hungrier—than others. Some are leaders, some are followers. And some, my favourites, seem to be just a little different. These are birds that, in my day, would have been unfortunately labeled "slow." Noisily bossed to the periphery, these poor guys never get first crack at the peanuts. They genially hop about, looking for a friend or a stray sunflower seed. Happy, it seems, just to be included, even if it's only a rebuke or scolding from some pushy, fat blue jay.

I've no doubt these little goofs would land on or near a cat if they thought it might want to be pals. These birds, usually tiny chickadees or juncos, don't even seem capable of dressing themselves properly. They have comically misplaced feathers jutting from the tops of their heads or tails, giving the impression they slept in or were rushed getting here. They are, I suppose, bird nerds.

As I say though, I marvel at them, all of them, especially these hardy few who winter over while hordes of their glamour-seeking, fair-weather brethren bail to warmer climes. If you were a bird in a jam, who would you want as your wingman? Some puffed up dandy of an oriole who's never had to peck his way through a sheet of ice so he could take a freezing bath in the morning? Or a feisty little redpoll who'd be happy just to scrounge some day-old bird seed when the mercury's so low you'd think your beak would fall off?

The other wonderful and astonishing thing about birds is that all they seem to do is make the world a prettier place. In the cold, cloudy grey of deepest winter, when most of us are trudging along, head down and miserable, they sing. For that one, lovely gift alone, all of us should put out a little seed.

GIRL'S A FAN EVEN THOUGH
LITTLE MOSQUE CHARACTER UNSYMPATHETIC

My wife and I were out with friends last week, eating at an Indian restaurant in Toronto. We were having a ball. Great food, great company, great conversation.

Midway through our meal I noticed movement beside me and looked over to see a little girl of maybe six or seven years old, her dad standing with her, politely waiting for my attention. I smiled at her. She giggled and buried her face in her father's legs. He leaned over and whispered for her to, "Tell him what you wanted to say…"

She fixed two beautiful brown eyes on me, then shyly stammered out, "I really like you on your television show."

"Tell him what show it is, honey…"

"*Little Mosque on the Prairie.*"

I was delighted. Doubly so because this little girl, her dad and her mom, who had demurely remained at their table in a lovely blue hijab, were quite obviously Muslim. I also had to laugh out loud. My character, Fred Tupper, is a red-necked, fear-mongering, xenophobic boob. I like to think of him as kind of a lovable xenophobic boob—but still.

"You've seen me on that show and you still wanted to come and say hello?"

She nodded and with a smile and another giggle, completely stole those parts of my heart she didn't already possess.

I never tire of getting recognized in public. Canadians are inevitably painfully polite about approaching their celebrities, plus I've always keenly paid attention to that little voice in my head that warns of the day when nobody will care who I am or what I've done. Enjoy it while you have it, buster.

I have to say though that there was an enormously important difference between the dozens of people over the years who have approached me to say such kind things as, "Hey, I saw you in *Cop Killer XXIIV*" or "Say, weren't you 'Dead Security Guard No. Four' in *The Thing That Came From a Bad Place That Wasn't Earth?*" or even, "Love your underwear commercial"…and this little girl's simple message.

For the first time in 20 plus years, I felt like something I'd done on TV mattered. I felt like, in my own small over-acting, mugging-for-the-camera way, I had built (or at least *helped* build) a bridge—a much needed bridge over some very troubled waters.

That little girl, I am sure, had no idea how important her words were to me. But, she made my night. She made me feel proud.

I don't know if you've flipped through the *TV Guide* recently but, to my way of thinking, there's not a whole lot in there to be proud of. I don't think I'd have experienced nearly the same joy if some little girl, Muslim or otherwise, had approached my table and said, "I'm so glad you're still on the island," or "I saw you on *Springer*. Your girlfriend's a skank," or even "Nice butt."

But last night, as my little friend and her dad toddled back to their table and I returned to my butter chicken, I felt wonderfully happy to be a part of something that, to a particular group of people anyway, is more than just 22 minutes and a laugh track.

As I say, enjoy it while you have it buster.

Bracelet a Reminder of What's Truly Important in Life

I have a silver bracelet that is very important to me. I don't really like wearing a bracelet. I've never really considered myself a bracelet kind of guy. Bracelet guys have always been like necklace guys in my books. They drive snazzy cars and wear loads of cologne. They get married a lot—mostly to women with winter tans and names like Crystal, Tiffany or Chantal; women who dig snazzy cars and cologne. I could never pull that off. I don't think women named Crystal, Tiffany or Chantal dig guys who flood rinks and kiss their dogs on the lips.

I know that my own wife, whose name is nowhere close to Crystal or any other mineral, kind of hates my bracelet. She knows it's important to me though and bites her tongue. She's a good friend. Still, I'm fairly sure there would be an immediate and frank discussion if I ever came home in a snazzy car or came downstairs reeking of something called Bilge pour l'homme.

My bracelet is important because it is a reminder. On it are written seven words that have become lifesavers for me, "Nothing is worth more than this day." That's it. That's all. "Nothing is worth more than this day."

Each morning when I get up and get dressed, regardless of what worry or issue or concern is careening around inside my head, when I reach for this silver bracelet I am reminded to put the brakes on for just a moment and realign my attitude for the day.

I am reminded that I had cancer and am still here and that others are not. I am reminded to take a look around me at my warm house, my soft bed, my warm, soft wife, my beautiful children, and all the million things waiting to be enjoyed in this day I've just been given.

You might find it hard to believe someone who has had a life-threatening disease could ever forget to be in love with this precious thing called existence. But it happens.

You get better, your hair grows back and you put your toes into the stream of life once more. If you're not really strong on your feet, however, you soon find yourself swiftly sucked along by the same old current of worry, fear and pettiness that defined your existence prior to your tumour. I think it's called human nature.

I wish it were human nature for all of us to awaken to each day thrilled with its possibilities and delights, eager and excited to embrace the joy awaiting us. But it is not. At least not in my neck of the woods. Instead, most of us need a reminder.

There may have been a time in our rural past when we awakened and walked outside to be greeted by the glory of nature. The beauty of the fields, flowers, woods and sky loudly proclaimed how precious the day was. But most of us have a difficult time finding enlightenment in the glow of the TV or the dashboard lights or the clock alarm LED blinking 5 a.m. Hence, the bracelet.

You may not want to be a bracelet guy. I'd understand if you didn't. There are only so many Tiffanys and Chantals to go round, after all. Still, I hope you can find something somewhere that will spark you to reset your compass every morning. It's made all the difference in the world to me. And it's cheaper than cologne.

No Matter What, in the End, You Have to Do What Feels Right

I was hanging out in an airport recently, waiting to board my flight, trying to shake the Interpol guys on my tail, when I walked past one of those shoeshine stands. You know the ones where you sit way up high in full view of everybody passing by and put your brogues up on the stand so the guy can do his thing with the brush and cream?

There was a man sitting on this one, stereotypically reading the financial papers in a power suit, tie and $80 haircut. He had the furrowed brow of someone intent on crushing a small company or turfing orphans and widows out of a tenement. And I am sure, had the bylaws not disallowed it, he'd have been chomping on a stogie to boot.

He was also white. I include that detail only because the gentleman shining his shoes was not. He was a black man.

Now, call me old-fashioned, but that's just not something I could ever do. For the life of me, I could not sit there on that throne, with thousands of people as witness and have a black man shine my shoes—regardless of what I was paying him; regardless of how happy he seemed to be. The entire setup is just such a vivid icon of a past most of us, I hope, are desperately trying to move beyond—the overseer seated high up while the low-status underling toils away at his feet. Yikes. All that's missing is a mint julep, riding crop and somebody singing "Zippadee-doo-dah." I don't care how dirty my shoes are, I'm not perpetuating that scenario.

Maybe I'm being overly sensitive. Maybe the guy up there with his boots on the stand was just trying to help out his fellow man by throwing a little business his way. Maybe. Still, I couldn't do it. For the same reason I could never have an Asian man pull me in a rickshaw or have a topless woman wash my car. Well, OK, maybe not a full wash. I think I could tolerate a light rinse and wax. But, like wearing your underwear backwards or borrowing another guy's cup at hockey, these things just feel wrong.

I suspect this perceived problem is just that—my perceived problem. The black man shining those shoes may well have been the happiest man in that airport—independent, self-actualized, free and beholden to no man, going home at the end of the day to his family, feeling good about working hard to support them.

Or he may have been one of millions trapped on the treadmill of miserable, threadbare existence. The trouble is, I really don't know. What I do know, in fact—what is sometimes the *only* thing I know—is that I have to do what makes me feel good, what I can happily live with. In the end, I suppose, that's what it always boils down to. Every day is about choices. Choosing to love or to hate, to respect or to humiliate, to listen or to ignore, crunchy or smooth.

All we can do is try to make good ones. And I'm convinced that if we do that—if we always reach for what feels good—then eventually, the whole world starts to feel better. Then we won't even care about our shoes.

What's in a Name? Everything When It Comes to Your Cash

Investment season is upon us. Many of us will want to salt away a little something for our retirement, putting the kids through school or pony-ing up hush money for an Internet indiscretion. The choices of where to put these hard-earned funds can be bewildering. Consequently, the employ of a good, sound financial adviser is often the difference be-tween retiring to a Caribbean villa or a tent trailer in Keswick. The question is, with so many options out there, so many smiling faces knocking on your door, how do you know you're in good hands?

Well, as a self-employed artist with the financial stability of a chip truck and business acumen that would make Britney Spears look like a Rothschild, I've had to take certain steps to insure I'm not taken advantage of. To that end, I've developed what I think is a foolproof system for evaluating money men. If you employ even half of these handy tips, you can rest assured you're getting good bang for your bucks.

First, unlike the greater world outside of high finance, stereotypes in the money arena are everything. Get a bald guy. Preferably with horn-rimmed glasses. No hair equals worry and that's good. You don't want some clown with Hollywood good looks and locks like Fabio. That guy has obviously chiselled so many customers out of their savings that he hasn't a care in the world.

You want the guy who is fretting over your portfolio so much that you practically see the follicles leaping off his scalp. Likewise with the glasses. You don't develop poor eyesight by ignoring fine print. You want a stickler. The worse the guy's peepers, the better. Although I would pull up just this side of legally blind.

Of equal import to looks is a name. Again, these rules seldom apply in the outside world, but in the investment racket they're surefire. Almost without question avoid people with single syllable handles. Ron, Biff, Vance—these are not financial advisers. These are car salesmen and while it might be fun to go toe-to-toe with one of them over some free rust-proofing, handing them carte blanche with your fiscal future will almost certainly land you in a boarding house eating a plateful of cat food.

Polysyllabic is your safest and best bet. Stick with your Miltons, your Cliffords, your Kenneths. And if at any time any one of these asks you to please refer to him as Milt, Cliff or Ken, show him the door. A word to the wise—certain unsavory types have cottoned to this trend and have attempted to dupe unsuspecting investors with grandiose titles like Napoleon, Nebuchadrezzar and Solomon. Generally, if your adviser has a name that sounds like he may have at one time ruled the known world, I would give him a pass.

Finally, I like to know a great deal about my adviser's personal life. I see nothing untoward in a thorough getting-to-know-you session followed by a discreet phone call to Interpol. In the event you discover that your potential money manager has a thing for leather or pudding-wrestling or perhaps runs a website dedicated to the *Partridge Family*, so much the better. Nothing keeps the ledger cleaner than a little something in the closet you can use on a rainy day.

Follow these simple rules and your golden years are sure to be well in the black.

Children a Sure Sign of How Time Flies

Sometimes, especially in moments of great stillness or, for instance, when my agent hasn't called in a week or so, I am vividly aware of the arc of my life.

I can almost see it all trailing out behind me in a splendid, gentle curve with me, in my current moment, sitting happily at the apogee. I had one of these moments last evening as, at the end of a pleasant walk, I stood, gazing up into a clear, star-filled sky and breathed in the crystalline silence of my little town in winter.

Looking back along that arc I realize that certain signposts have disappeared from view. My backyard, I notice, is no longer filled, as it once was, with snow forts and tiny boot prints. The drifts there remain unspoiled and strangely barren, save for a snow sculpture of a huge chair and ottoman. At least my wife still likes to play in the snow.

The tree fort, too, is gone. Only a ghostly, rusting bike wheel nailed high up in the branches remains as witness to the burning imaginations that once played there. I am filled, briefly, with a sadness, a parent's lament to a lost, magical time.

But a further glance at the arc and I am reminded that nothing is ever really lost. Just changing—ever changing. There are new signposts springing up everywhere; informing me of where I am now and where I may be heading.

At times they appear so suddenly I find myself banging into them. Tree forts and snow forts and boot prints have been replaced by mp3 players and amps and drum kits. Pleasant Sunday car outings are now nervous, tongue-biting rides beside teen drivers; parental boots straining at phantom brake pedals.

The family room no longer rings with the sound of rolling dice and rousing board games, but the coy laughter of mascara-painted girls… sitting beside and sometimes on top of boys. Some signposts take a little more getting used to than others.

Finally, babysitters and adult nights out have been replaced by popcorn-munching and movie-watching—my wife and I trying in vain to keep each other conscious as we await the safe return of our maddeningly nocturnal offspring. And when they finally do go to bed, *Goodnight Moon* and *Where the Wild Things Are* gather dust on the bookshelf; my reading with children now confined to wrestling through a high school course prospectus.

One of the interesting and frankly terrifying things about raising children is that, like living, breathing sundials, they mark the passage of our lives.

I imagine people who live without children must be in a kind of perpetual stasis, like living in a home with no mirrors. Not a bad thing, mind you, for until I had a teenager under my roof, I had always felt like I was still 16 or 17 in many ways. But you cannot help but feel a little older, feel time slipping by, when you sit down at breakfast and they're suddenly taller than you, when yours are the smallest shoes on the mat—when the signposts are flying by. That's when the arc appears.

Still, it's comforting. I like my life. I like where I've been and I look forward to what lies ahead. I like the journey I'm on. And isn't that the real trick, after all? To enjoy the ride.

TOO MANY PEOPLE POINTING OUT THE OBVIOUS ON OUR DIME

Do you, like me, find yourself shaking your head several mornings a week as you hear the results of the latest study revealing such world-rocking truths as smoking is detrimental to your health, or that people who eat poorly tend to be overweight, or that exercise is, in fact, good for you? Is it just me, or does it seem like millions of dollars, usually taxpayers' dollars, are yearly being flushed down the dumper on projects designed to prove what most of us who can dress ourselves already know?

Alcohol consumption during pregnancy is not a good idea. Seat belts save lives. The earth is round. Yeah, OK...kinda already figured that one out myself, thanks.

I can only assume that there are a great many people making a dandy little living pointing out the obvious in a great many thousand-page reports. And frankly, I think I'd like a piece of that action. If someone wants to float me a multi-million dollar research grant, I'll happily put my acting career on hold for a few years to study any number of ridiculously obvious tenets.

As a result of intensive study we can now conclusively state that pants keep your legs warm, women are more effective breast-feeders than men and asbestos pillows are bad for you. My work here is done.

I've no doubt, in fact, I desperately hope that there is a great deal of very important research being paid for in the world. We need to monitor the health of the planet, we need to keep an eye out for medical breakthroughs, we need to explore the universe. In my book that's all money well spent.

But do we really need a study to tell us that people who fill their grocery carts full of pop and chips tend to be as big as a house? That individuals who live in poverty tend to be less happy than those who don't? That nine out of 10 people who strapped a live cat to their head got scratched? Hello?

I am convinced that hard-wired into all of us at a cellular level is the requisite knowledge to look after ourselves and lead safe, happy lives. It's there. We know, deep down, that it's not a great idea to consume nothing but alcohol and fried food. We know that we'll live longer and happier lives if we exercise now and then. We know that strapping a live cat to our head is only funny some of the time. We understand these things. The problem is that we are human and that we don't always make good choices. But that's OK, too. It's called natural selection or, in more common parlance, vacuuming the gene pool. I don't think we need any more studies to point out our failings. We are aware of them. And sometimes we have to learn the hard way. That's why God invented paramedics.

Besides, how might our society look if the millions used to study and catalogue its ills were instead used to prevent them? An interesting question. Someone should do a study on that.

I hate the "check engine" light. It's like driving with an hysterical aunt. There's never any gentle warning or calm admonition. Never a "You might want to consider checking your oil" or "Hmmm, I think a belt needs tightening, but I wouldn't sweat it" or even "Compression is down a hair Phil, just so's you know." Instead it's full-on panic—battle stations, battle stations!

I'm sure, were there not some law preventing it, the "check engine" light would be accompanied by a deafening claxon or perhaps a Shelley Winters sound-alike shrieking "We're all gonna die! We're all gonna die!"

And the automobile manual, far from clarifying things with a level-headed explanation, actually throws gasoline on the fire. In bold-face type it makes it horrifyingly clear your life is hanging by a thread, "If check engine light indicator is on, drive directly to dealership or garage," with a firmly implied "Good luck, chump."

It's only a hair away from advising you to jump from the vehicle immediately. And that drive to the garage or dealership is always fun, isn't it? Driving any distance with the "check engine" light on is like toodling along with a twitchy-thumbed suicide bomber sitting in the passenger seat. As long as that damned light is on there's a more than good chance the vehicle will burst into a fiery ball of death at any moment.

The icon itself, a simple amber or red engine block, is ridiculously misleading. For all the terrible weight of the message, it should really flash a skull and crossbones. Even the nuclear radiation sign would be more fitting.

Of course, because you don't want to die or run the risk of taking others out with you as your car careens out of control with you holding a dislodged steering wheel in your hands, you dutifully follow instructions and drive to the nearest dealership or garage. Neither of which, by the by, is ever *near* anything. Nothing is ever close by when you're suddenly driving with a trunk full of nitroglycerin.

Now, should you actually survive the journey to the shop, the mechanic inevitably snaps what amounts to a five hundred dollar-an-hour auto-colonoscope onto your vehicle and you discover that the world isn't, in fact, coming to an end. Civilization as we know it will continue, provided you top up your windshield wiper fluid. Phew. That one was close.

It might be nice if, as a gesture of apology, the makers of any vehicle with the crazy-making "check engine" light also installed its antithesis. Call it a "driver stroke indicator" or "ev'ry t'ings irie light" or even a "swell" button.

We've been so conditioned to freak whenever something on our dash lights up that might it not be a lovely change if occasionally we received not a warning but an affirmation?

Bing. "This little baby is running like a top, Doug."

Bing. "Nancy, that was a three-point turn made in heaven."

Bing. "Nice call on those snow tires Vic, and don't you listen to the guys at the office, that dickey looks cool."

I'd pay for something like that.

Hanging Private Parts From Vehicles a Tad Distracting

I've noticed a rather disturbing trend lately in the world of automotive accessories. In one week of commuting to Toronto and back I saw one car with a pair of breasts hanging from his rearview mirror and two, count 'em, *two* pickups with (and trust me, I'm having difficulty swallowing as I type this) a set of testicles hanging from the bumper hitch. It's just occurred to me that that is the first time in many years of writing that I've ever used the words testicles and bumper hitch in the same sentence. We live in strange times indeed.

But truth, it seems, is stranger than fiction. I'm not sure what kind of a message one gives to the world when one hangs a pair of breasts from one's rearview mirror. And these were not key chain-sized, cute, novelty breasts. These were at least the size of the ubiquitous fuzzy dice most often found adorning vehicles impounded in street-racing incidents. The only saving grace is that the breasts were not fuzzy. That would've induced more difficulty swallowing, I am sure.

I can understand how some men would enjoy a display of this nature. I, however, could not have a set of boobs hanging from my rearview mirror or anywhere in my car frankly. Unable to take my eyes off them, I would crash the vehicle. I would not make it out of the driveway. It's that simple. I know my limitations. This is one of the reasons when I ride with my wife, I generally ask her to drive.

The second apparition—the auto scrotum, as it were—is a much trickier phenomenon to explain. Even as a male, I have seldom seen a more off-putting image than a larger-than-life set of knackers swinging boldly to and fro on the back of a truck. And this was in the winter-time. I can only assume that in the warmer weather they will be even larger.

More arresting is the fact that one of these trucks was a commer-cial vehicle! Who was the marketing genius who thought a pair of bumper bollocks would be good for business? Nothing sets the house-wife at ease faster than seeing that on the back of the plumber's van. And while we're at it, if these things are sold in sets, I don't even want to think about what the hood ornament looks like. Yikes.

Also, and I hate to even conjure this image, but at some point in time it stands to reason, from a purely statistical point of view, that one of these vehicles will be rear-ended. The chain reaction of accidents set off from male drivers witnessing this event will be catastrophic.

The sympathetic agony felt by watching even a metal set of cojones crushed between the weight of two vehicles would create a passing-out radius of five miles at least.

On the upside, there'd be a lot of happy women enjoying a clear road for a change.

STUPID PET TRICKS ARE A PART OF EVERYDAY EXISTENCE

I just spent the better part of the morning trying to get a frozen squirrel out of the bottom of my downspout. So much for the life of a celebrity. I was chipping away at the gruesome little rodent-sicle and found myself wondering if John Wayne or Gregory Peck ever had to do this kind of thing. Somehow I don't think so. Richard Gere had a thing for rodents, I recall, but I don't remember a downspout being involved.

Getting a squirrel out of your downspout is not as cut and dried as you might think. And of course, it begs the question "How did he get in there in the first place?" I've considered several scenarios but I think the closest explanation involves said squirrel, on my roof, poised precariously above the downspout, uttering the phrase "Hey fellas, watch this!"

No squirrel can be said to be smart, and this particular fellow, I can only assume, was nowhere near the head of his class. It seems only reasonable, after all, that Mother Nature, on occasion, creates a moron in the animal kingdom. Why should all the idiots be human only?

If we slow down and take a little more heed of the natural world around us we begin to see abundant evidence of this shallow end of the animal gene pool. The one bird in a flock of 100 who flies into a window. The myopic dragonfly who manages to find the only car grill in thousands of miles of open prairie. The mouse that nests in the cozy confines of a shotgun barrel.

At a downtown rooftop party I once witnessed a dog happily leap over the edge of the building in pursuit of an errantly thrown ball.

Miraculously, a canvas awning three stories below broke his fall and he was completely unharmed. Lucky for him there was no downspout.

Some animals, in fact entire breeds of creatures, seem so completely stupid that they defy Darwin by their very existence.

I have yet to see a mourning dove, for instance, that didn't appear to be wearing the avian equivalent of a dunce cap.

Their call, I think, should not be a "coo" so much as a "huh?" Sheep have the IQ of a bran muffin. In fact, had sheep not been domesticated all those years ago, does anyone really think these woolly blobs of panic would still be around? Are you kidding? Sheep have two speeds—graze and cripes! These ovine psychotics have convinced themselves that if we could, human beings would eat lamb three times a day, seven nights a week.

Have you ever witnessed a herd of sheep destroying a patch of mint? Mint sauce is a sheep's worst enemy. And deer, for all their athletic grace and beauty are unquestionably the Britney Spears of the animal kingdom. If deer had thumbs I have no doubt we would see them riding snowmobiles over thin ice well into spring.

But as I say, if animals sometimes display idiotic behaviour, they are only mimicking their human counterparts. We have a corner on stupid. And the only reason no one has ever had to chip a man out of a downspout is because we wouldn't fit.

YOU'VE GOT TO RECONNECT WITH YOUR IMAGINATION

I have always endeavoured to take care of myself. I walk a great deal, ride the bike, play hockey, snowshoe, even tie myself in knots with a little yoga now and then. I put a great deal of stock in the old adage "Use it or lose it." Although a more appropriate maxim for my financial fitness might be "Use it *and* lose it."

Still, I think it's important to put the body to work—if for no other reason than I don't want to end up looking like Jabba the Hutt; needing the jaws of life to get into my automobile.

Recently, however, I've realized that for all of my physical activity, there's a part of me that's been sorely neglected to the point of atrophy—my imagination.

I wonder if you're in the same boat. I suspect many of us are.

Do you recall, as a child, how easy it was to picture yourself being, doing or having anything at all in this or any other world?

Can you remember that time when the boundaries of your life seemed absolutely limitless? When you lived without fear or worry or self-doubt? When fantasy was as much a part of your daily clothing as socks and underwear? I can, but only barely. And I find that terribly upsetting.

One might think that as a creative artist my life would be full of imaginings. But it isn't. There's a great deal of thinking that goes on, lots of it wonderfully creative thinking, some of it hard, smoke coming out of the ears thinking. But it's thinking. And that's a very different animal from imagining. Thinking involves dealing with what you have. Imagining toys with what you might want. Very different animal.

I'm not sure when it started, when I suddenly began putting a cap on my dream bottle. No doubt it coincided with that time in my life when I decided I was an adult and should start behaving like one. Done deal. The plan had unfolded and it was just a matter of settling into it and seeing it out. No more fantasies, no more imagining other frontiers, other versions of me—*Neil 2.0*. That was it.

And what occurs then, when we no longer steer our ships in the direction of our dreams? Some of us drift aimlessly, tossed about by the waves around us, but most of us just tie the wheel off in the direction we've always been heading, letting our past define and thereby design our future.

We've always lived this way, thought these things, expected this stuff, so why should the future be any different? Well, why not? Why can't tomorrow be entirely different from today in a million wonderful ways?

I haven't been able to come up with a good reason why it shouldn't, other than I've always "thought" it should be the same. So I've decided to try an experiment. I'm going to start thinking less and imagining more. Or at least spend as much time dreaming as I do thinking. I'm going to wool-gather, blue-sky, moodle. All of those things we were taught not to do as kids. And I'm going to see if I can't get back some of the wonderful that, as a seven-year-old boy, I had planned for myself.

I met Andrew and his lovely wife, Marilyn, a couple of years ago at a cancer fundraiser. I had noticed this tall, completely bald guy making a lot of people laugh throughout the evening. I was hosting—you get to see a lot from up there at the podium. He seemed like an interesting guy even from up there. Later on I got a closer look and I noticed, for the first time, the large scars and slight indentations to Andrew's skull. This gentleman is intimately acquainted with surgery, I thought. At any rate, we were—through thought or design, fate or the finger of God— brought together and by night's end had made plans to meet again.

That's the way it often is in the cancer community. People don't waste time. There's not a lot of pussyfooters in the cancer world. Life is precious.

I discovered how very precious life is to my friend Andrew.

Here is a guy who has had, over a number of procedures, a very large chunk of his brain removed in a constant battle with cancer. And yet he, with approximately half his normal grey matter is, in my humble opinion, smarter than the leader of the United States. Andrew has been on more varieties of chemo than I can count. His bloodstream is like the Baskin Robbins of chemo. He has also outlived every dire prognosis given him. Statistics and current medical wisdom had him dead a couple of years ago. But he is still here and he is very much alive. He burns with life. He is a neat guy to stand beside. You can feel the heat.

So when I received what was for Andrew and his normally re- markably upbeat manor, a decidedly sad email, my heart broke. He has run out of his 31 flavours. There is no more chemo left to try and the cancer is growing. They are taking him off it. He has been told that his death is not imminent—but, as my dad says, "I wouldn't order any soft-boiled eggs."

He and Marilyn have had to arrange palliative care, make his own funeral arrangements and explain to his two tearful, angry children what is happening—all without coming completely undone himself.

I had cancer once, a very bad cancer. I looked down that black barrel a couple of times, but I was spared seeing the bullet with my name on it. I never got to the point where someone finally put a time-table on my life, where I went shopping for tombstones and epitaphs, where I envisioned, I mean really saw my kids without a dad. Andrew is there.

But, typically, he is there with his usual faith, courage, love and depthless humour. My overwhelming emotion upon receiving his email, besides a terrible heartache, was love. I was swallowed by love. My love for him and his family and greater still, the enormity of love that I knew was required for him to pen those hard, painful words to me.

And as hard as they are to read, they are a gift—a mighty gift. You put those words in your head, words from someone who is seeing the world and the beauty of it as clearly as anyone ever saw it and your own vision crisps up considerably. That kind of gift has an enormous price tag. Thank you for that, Andrew—and for so much more my friend.

The Final Stage—Jingling Loose Change in Your Pocket

I've been fairly successful at ignoring many of the signs that I am aging. The initial loss of hair, the subsequent greying of the hair, and then, as if Mother Nature were trying to compensate for the first bit, the ridiculous growing of hair on parts of the body that never had hair before—back, ears, nose.

None of those things, as I say though, really reached me. But just lately, as I approach my 48th year, certain behaviours have been cropping up, undeniable reminders that time is indeed passing and, more frighteningly, that I am turning into my dad.

Don't get me wrong. I love the old man. I could do far worse than walk in his footsteps. It's not the becoming like my dad that is alarming, it's the fact that such a metamorphosis is irrefutable evidence that I am no longer 16 or even 20.

For starters, I am becoming a pocket guy. As men age we find ourselves carrying a lot more stuff around with us. For this we need pockets. I used to wonder why my dad always wore cargo pants and a fishing vest around the place. I now understand. He needed all those pockets for his stuff.

What is this stuff? Difficult question. Beyond certain staples—pencils, pens, Swiss Army knives, eyeglass screwdriver-kits and combs, (for our backs) men's stuff varies from guy to guy.

As a younger man, I, for instance, used to be able to arrive home from work, hop out of the car and into the house in seconds. Everything I needed was either in my head or in my hand. Now I must sit in the car and gather my stuff.

Invariably I have an mp3 player and a cellphone to tuck away. I have an electronic voice recorder for storing ideas and thoughts which otherwise would seep out of my brain like water through weeping tile. I have my automatic garage-door opener, my car keys and of course the little thing I carry with me that allows my petroleum provider to know exactly where I am and what I am spending money on 24 hours a day.

I have glasses. Not one pair, but several. Like my kids and their indoor shoes, I have my car glasses and my indoor glasses. I also have my sunglasses and a hat. Whereas once upon a time I relished the feel of the sun on my naked head I now realize that radioactive fireball in the sky is, in fact, trying to kill me and I must take measures to protect myself.

I may have a travel mug and a book and very possibly a map because all of a sudden I am afraid I could get lost in this province that I've grown up in. Luckily I have a Swiss Army knife.

Depending on the weather and the time of the year there will be gloves, lozenges and perhaps a nasal mister. And of course, change. All men have pockets full of loose change. As we get older we learn the delightful art of jingling this with one hand in the pocket. That is the real sound of male maturity by the way. Whereas at one point a hand in the pocket had other things to toy with, we now play with our change. Whistling while jingling the change is the final stage.

Start doing that and you may as well be in a home.

Father's and Mother's Day Biggest Days of the Year

I sometimes wonder that, rather than Christmas, Hanukkah, Ramadan or any of the other momentous religious occasions, Mother's Day and Father's Day aren't the real biggies.

Who in this life, after all, is a more seminal part of our collective happiness equation than our parents? Whose is the first face we see? The first voice we hear? The first touch we feel?

Many of us may spend the last half of our lives desperately trying to emulate Jesus, Mohammed or the Buddha. But whose shoes are we trying to fill for that first part? Mom or Dad, usually.

Our parents, like it or not, are the gods of much of our lives. They have an enormous hand in shaping who and what we are, both physically and emotionally. And their choices to nurture us, feed us, stimulate us, support us or not, can, and very often do, make the difference between a lifetime of joy or struggle.

I recently read something about the difference between *growing* children and *raising* children.

Anybody can *grow* a child; the same way anyone can grow a hog or a horse or a cow. Feed it, water it, keep it clean and free of disease and it will grow to physical maturity. You can do the same with a human, of course. Many do. We've all met lots of full-grown, well-fed, immaculately clean, unhappy people.

To *raise* a child, on the other hand, is a very different process altogether. It involves far more than simply throwing money, groceries and laundry at the kid. We must throw ourselves into the bargain. We must put our hearts, minds and souls on full alert 24/7.

We must be ever watchful, ever mindful and ever caring about those people we created and to whom, therefore, we are eternally responsible. No easy task. And it never ends.

My own mother and father bent over backwards to see that myself and my five siblings were well fed, warm, clean and healthy for all the days we lived under their roof and then some. I thank them for that. But what I love them for and what I remember best are not the meals, new shoes or trips to the doctor but the million other things that they did not out of duty, but out of love.

I remember my mother never failing to kiss me good night, even well into my teens, when entry into my bedroom meant donning some kind of respiratory aid. I remember butterscotch Laura Secord suckers—just because.

I remember my father picking me up and tossing me what felt like miles high before gleefully landing in the surf of Wasaga Beach. Forty odd years later, I remember him still holding me up, my arm around his shoulders, as we shuffled up and down a hospital corridor, my belly full of staples.

When I call my folks, both now in their 80s, the conversation very often surrounds the weather, current events, their health, but inevitably, and without fail, it will come around to me, my brothers and my sister...their children. They are, and always will be, our parents. We are all grown but as long as they are alive, they will, in their way, still be raising us.

METAL CONCERT A REVELATION TO THIS MIDDLE-AGED CHAPERONE

I went to my first "metal" concert last week. Well, I'm generalizing. My children are quick to inform me, with remarkable condescension, that there are, in fact, several important subspecies, classes and perhaps even phylum of metal—thrash, grind and death metal. All three cheery varieties made their various discordant assaults on my eardrums that night. And it was great—really.

I was there in two capacities—as chaperone/narc/the man, and parent to a drummer in one of the bands. Both roles proved life-changing.

At the beginning of the night I stood at the base of the stairs leading up to the auditorium. Kids purchased tickets then filed past my area. My tasks were simple—make sure no one snuck in or left through the door behind me and check all backpacks and bags for unpurchased food, drink and assorted tools of Satan.

If you want to feel immediately old and supremely square, ask a kid with spiked hair, black lipstick and more piercings than a Ubangi chieftain, if you can look in her bag. These kids are well practiced in the art of "harrumph." From the looks I got, I might as well have been wearing an SS uniform.

Then again, I thought, can you really blame them? I don't enjoy having some airport security geek paw over my stuff. Guilty until proven innocent has never been a great way to win friends. And, truth be told, none of the kids had anything more potent than bottled water with them. Thus began my own metamorphosis. I started to really like these kids…even understand them a bit. One of the highlights of my night was getting a smile from a girl with "Bite Me" tattooed on her breast. You don't forget stuff like that.

The heart of a metal concert, aside from the music, which frankly is like walking through a wood shop where every other lathe is badly out of calibration, is the mosh pit. Imagine sumo wrestling on the Bloor subway platform during rush hour and you pretty much have it.

Kids of all shapes and sizes jumping, hopping, spinning and bumping into one another like frenzied dervishes. And yet it's not at all violent. At least this one wasn't. If anything, it was inclusive—an equal opportunity bruising.

Suzanne and I watched from the safety of the balcony as our youngest son dove into the frantic matrix of bodies again and again and was happily, even proudly, spit out every time like a 13-year-old ping-pong ball. Amazing.

But for me, the real wonder of the night was watching my oldest, drummer for the headlining band, walk onto the stage, and to the roar of a couple hundred kids, light into a drum solo that blew the doors off the place. I felt a thrill go through me then, the likes of which I haven't felt since I first laid eyes on him.

I used to quietly lament the fact that, as an ex-jock, my kid wasn't really all that into sports. I had envisioned myself at his games, supporting him, coaching him, heart-to-hearts in the car after the loss— the whole nine yards.

I was a selfish jerk and thank God I kept those thoughts to myself. Our children will show us their gifts when they are ready. And when they do, if we have the eyes and hearts to see them, we will be blessed a thousand-fold by the wonder of it.

Bucking Bronco Makes his Debut on the Horses

I've started taking *horseback-riding* lessons. Although those of us in the know, the horsey set, simply call them *riding* lessons. Why? For the same arcane reason I would never call Judy my *horseback-riding* instructor. If I want to be cool and possibly score an invitation back to Chas and Lauren's place for a gin and tonic after polo, I have learned to casually refer to her as my *riding* instructor.

Aside from all the physical mechanics involved in learning to happily and safely sit atop a seven-foot high, 1,200 pound animal, even more important are those bits of curricula not found in the textbooks. Those vital do's and don'ts one can pick up only by watching and listening. And believe me, a misstep in this area can be every bit as painful as being thrown from the saddle. Nothing smarts like a bruised ego.

Luckily for me, my wife is a rider of some experience and she is more than happy to point out my gaffs on such occasions.

For instance, one of the first things we riders learn to do, even before leaping aboard Old Thunder is to clean the horse's hooves. This involves holding the animal's often wet, often mucky, often manure-laden foot in one hand while scraping off the aforementioned guck with a pick. After a couple of weeks of getting my dainty actor's hands all dirty doing this, I decided to pop into a tack shop and pick myself up a handsome pair of butter-soft, doeskin roping gloves. Just the ticket, I thought, for keeping the hands clean. Plus, I imagined, it'll surely only be another lesson or two before we cover roping, branding and perhaps shooting from the saddle. I'll want to be prepared.

Tickled with my purchase and not a little flushed with how cool I would look with my new gloves on, I showed my wife. When she eventually was able to see again through her tears of laughter, she pointed out to me that gloves were a no-no. Wearing gloves to riding lessons, she made it clear, was akin to showing up to your first golf lesson with a caddie in tow or in-line skating with a full-face motorcycle helmet. It spelled doofus in bold letters.

Since I have started my riding lessons, my wife has been laughing a lot. She's really enjoying herself. Good thing for me she happens to love doofuses. Still, I can't help myself. For the same reasons that I became an actor and a writer, I cannot put a pair of cowboy boots on and not want to act and talk like a cowboy.

It took some of Suzanne's very best scowls to get me to stop swaggering. And believe me, I had to muster every ounce of self-discipline in my body to purchase a proper riding helmet and not a totally cool black Stetson with silver braid on it. If they'd sold pearl-handled six-shooters I'd have maxed out my credit card. That would've been a tough return, "Um, my wife says I can't have these."

One of the benefits of learning new things—of going outside our comfort zones—is that if we happen to be riding one, we must get off our high horse for a while. We must shelve the ego. Sometimes difficult, but good for us. Plus, it's an endless source of amusement for our spouses. And laughter, they say, is good for a marriage.

Dog Days of Spring Lead to Unpleasant Surprise

The family and I spent a weekend downtown recently. A good friend kindly offered to look after the dog for us while we were away. We were only going to be gone for an afternoon, a night and the next morning. But when your pooch is the canine equivalent of a cross between Liberace and Mariah Carey, you have to take steps.

He knew we were going of course. He knew it from the moment we got up that morning. I'm not sure how dogs do this but the instant the idea of a car ride or the word "walk" is even formed in your thoughts, they are already in the vehicle or standing at the door, tail wagging expectantly. Our current dog, as I have alluded, is somewhat on the needy side. He is fanatically neat, a snappy dresser, has very little time for puppies or children and will only cuddle if I put show tunes on.

He was found, the animal shelter folks told us, abandoned at the side of the road. I can only assume that this was the result of some dispute between he and the rest of the doggie boy-band he'd been touring with. He is, if nothing else, a diva. This is why, again, careful measures must be taken to make sure he is tended to if we have to be away for even the briefest period.

You see, the wonderful and unfortunately often annoying thing about dogs—and dolphins too, I imagine, although I've never owned one—is their sentience.

They are just too damn smart for their own good. And married to all of that intelligence is a good deal of guile. And though you may take all the steps and measures in the world to make sure he is kept comfortable and fed and played with and that, God forbid, his wet, black nose does not get out of joint, sometimes it's just not enough.

Dogs hold grudges. After being away for a week, I once had an English Mastiff drop a sizeable bowel movement into my gym bag. No easy feat. He was a very big dog and it was a very small bag. And this was an animal with a fair amount of self-confidence. Needy dogs, on the other hand, whack-job divas, go even further. They understand that, in the words of Oscar Wilde, "Revenge is a dish best served cold."

And so it came to pass that we arrived home from our junket to the city and, after a brief inspection, everything looked just fine. No tattered pillows, no surprises on the rug and Judy Garland happily and apparently innocently wagging his tail at our return. There was even, after my humming a few bars of a Streisand ditty, the briefest of cuddles. All's well that ends well.

I was tired that night—bone tired. We had done a lot of walking downtown and I was thoroughly looking forward to some sleep time. Yawning pleasantly, I threw back the comforter, got into bed and slid my feet down into the cool sheets. Correction, the cold sheets. The cold, wet sheets. The cold, wet, urine-soaked sheets. Message received and noted.

Neil Crone has been a fixture in Canadian television for years, starring in such shows as *Wind at My Back* and CBC's award-winning *Little Mosque on the Prairie*. Besides acting and public speaking, Neil is a prolific writer. In addition to his weekly column in select Metroland newspapers entitled "Enter Laughing" Neil has written two children's books. The first, *Who Farted? Stories in Verse for Big & Little Kids* is a fun and whimsical collection of children's poetry. The second, *The Farmers' Secret Midnight Dance* is a beautiful story of magic and discovery. Both books are illustrated by Canadian cartoonist, Wes Tyrell.

Neil's books are published by Wintertickle Press and are available online and in fine book-selling establishments—independent and otherwise.

To learn more about Neil Crone, please feel free to check out his website at **www.neilcrone.com**.

CPSIA information can be obtained at www.ICGtesting.com
Printed in the USA
LVOW01s1427240114

370874LV00018B/1001/P